THE JEWS– PEOPLE OF THE FUTURE

Ulf Ekman

Word of Life Publications

THE JEWS—PEOPLE OF THE FUTURE
First published in English, 1993

ISBN 91 7866 210 9
ISBN 1 884017 04 5 USA

Original Swedish edition, copyright © 1992
Ulf Ekman. All rights reserved

English translation, copyright © 1993 Ulf Ekman

Printed in Finland for Word of Life Publications
by TryckPartner AB

Word of Life Publications
Box 17, S-751 03 Uppsala, Sweden
Box 46108, Minneapolis, MN 55446, USA
Box 641, Marine Parade, Singapore 9144

Acknowledgments
Unless otherwise indicated, Scripture quotations are
from the *Holy Bible, New International Version*,
copyright © 1973, 1978, 1984 International Bible Society.
Used by permission of Zondervan Bible Publishers

Other Scripture quotations are from the *New King
James Version* of the Bible NKJV, copyright © 1979, 1980,
1982 Thomas Nelson, Inc.; *The Living Bible* TLB,
copyright © 1971 Tyndale House Publishers

Dedication

*To Harry Hurwitz, a man whose
dedication to his people has taught me
more than words can describe*

Contents

Foreword

The discovery of what the Bible says about Israel revolutionized my spiritual life.

Israel is not simply a museum of past religious events but an eminent site in ancient history. This country is the scene of history's center, its climax and its close.

Unfortunately, ignorance of God's plans for the land of Israel and the Jews veils the eyes of all too many people. Such ignorance could prove fatal in the future, being a breeding ground for prejudice and the cause of many wrong decisions.

Today, it is crucial for us to have a clear understanding of God's dealings with His chosen people. We must take a stand with the people of God and their land, Israel. It would be impossible to write about it in a single volume. Therefore, this book simply attempts to clarify basic facts to enable us to understand more easily God's dealings with His people.

It is my desire that God will fill your heart with a love for what He loves, and a conviction of the importance of what He counts important; namely, His land and His people. As you receive this, the future will be much clearer to you, and your life will be greatly blessed.

God bless you!

Ulf Ekman

1

The People

The Lord has declared this day that you are his people, his treasured possession as he promised, and that you are to keep all his commands. He has declared that He will set you in praise, fame and honor high above all the nations he has made and that you will be a people holy to the Lord your God, as he promised (Deut 26:18-19).

The Lord will establish you as his holy people, as he promised you on oath, if you keep the commands of the Lord your God and walk in his ways. Then all the peoples on earth will see that you are called by the name of the Lord, and they will fear you (Deut 28:9-10).

Abraham was a central figure in God's plan of blessing for all mankind. He was to become the forefather of God's chosen people, the Jews, and God had a land ready for them: Israel.

These people, separate and holy to God, were to be his channel for blessing and salvation to all mankind. The world would be restored through the Jews. Therefore God said to Abraham, when he called him out of Ur of the Chaldeans, *I will make you into a great nation and I will bless you* (Gen 12:2). This is also why God told him, *I am God Almighty: walk before me and be blameless* (Gen 17:1).

Eventually, after years of waiting, Abraham's son was born and Isaac received the same promise and blessing to become a great nation. Jacob, one of Isaac's sons, also became heir of the promise. Jacob himself had twelve sons, one of whom, Joseph, was sold into slavery by his older brothers. They then persuaded their father that Joseph had been killed.

Later, when he discovered that Joseph was not dead, but was, in fact, alive and regent of Egypt, Jacob moved there with the entire family clan. Then they numbered 70 persons in total. The family had lived as foreigners in Canaan, though all the time holding firm to the promise that the land was their divine inheritance.

When Jacob left for Egypt, it was with the assurance that it would not be forever, for God had said to Abraham decades earlier, *Know for certain that your descendants will be strangers in a country not their own* (Egypt), *and they will be enslaved and mistreated four hundred years. But I will punish the nation they serve as slaves, and afterward they will come out with great possessions* (Gen 15:13-14).

So Egypt was not Jacob's land, but it was only the place where he and his family would increase to become a people. *I am God, the God of your father,* God said to him (Gen 46:3). *Do not be afraid to go down to Egypt, for I will make you into a great nation there.*

Egypt was to be the place where Jacob's twelve sons and their families would grow into twelve tribes, and then into a nation. The Bible tells us in Exodus 1:7, *The Israelites...became exceedingly numerous, so that the land was filled with them.*

At this point, however, a new Pharaoh arose who began to persecute them. As long as they had only been insignificant in number, they were looked upon with disdain (and sometimes with hatred) and as of no consequence whatever. Yet when they began to multiply, they were regarded as a threat but not to territorial boundaries or politics. The danger was of another kind. It was spiritual.

As the tribes increased, they became what God wanted them to be, and entered the calling He had for them. They became His instrument for blessing mankind—and they immediately encountered spiritual resistance!

However, despite intense opposition, nothing could stop the promises of God from being fulfilled. These promises included their total liberation. True, God had led them to Egypt, but it was not their land, and He had promised to lead them out again. In Exodus 2:23-25, we read an account of what happened during this time:

> During that long period, the king of Egypt died. The Israelites groaned in their slavery and cried out, and their cry for help because of their slavery went up to God. God heard their groaning and he remembered his covenant with Abraham, with Isaac and with Jacob. So God looked on the Israelites and was concerned about them.

The Exodus

When God sent Moses and delivered His people from Egypt, He did it through signs, wonders and mighty acts. The greatest miracle in the Old Testament is God's supernatural liberation of His people. In the heat of Egypt's persecution, the Israelites had been welded together. Then as they pressed through the passage in the Red Sea, they were formed into one body, and the nation of Israel was born.

The nature of their deliverance makes them what they are—God's own people. He loves and cares for them, and He revealed it by His stunning rescue campaign, Operation Exodus. His people walked out of Egypt in prosperity and health, as their God did the impossible for them.

At the same time, just as God had told Abraham, He judged the nation that had tormented and persecuted Israel. First, ten plagues covered their land, and then the waters of the Red Sea covered and drowned Egypt's pursuing army (Ex 14).

Though Moses had repeatedly held audience with Pharaoh, declaring, *This is what the Lord says: Let my people go, so that they may worship me* (Ex 8:1); it was not until after the ten plagues had wreaked havoc in the land of Egypt that he was ready to release them!

Satan had used Pharaoh to try to stop the plan of God. This attack centered on three areas:

1. **The people**—Israel was not to become a strong nation.

2. **The promise (the land)**—Israel was not to enter into her God-given inheritance.

3. **The purpose**—Israel was not to worship God.

These areas were central to God's purposes. He wanted a people He could call His own, "my people." This was His purpose for forming them into a nation and for promising them land. He wanted them to honor and worship Him. He wanted them to live for Him. The Israelites were to be totally separated for this service to Him.

God needed a people here on earth through whom **He** could be glorified. He wanted to show them and every other nation who He is. He wanted a people through whom He could do His mighty acts and through whom His plans and purposes on earth could be realized.

This is the reason for God's deep concern for His people Israel. This is why He feels both anger and sorrow at their disobedience. It is also why satanic resistance against the nation is so intense. If the people fail, God fails. If the people could be stopped, seduced or stamped out, so could God's plan of salvation. Such is God's commitment to His chosen people.

The divine calling to the children of Israel began in earnest with their exodus from Egypt. They were told by the Lord never to forget their liberation, but to remember it forever. *This is a day you are to commemorate. For the generations to come you shall celebrate it as a festival to the Lord—a lasting ordinance* (Ex 12:14).

The Passover

With these words, God commanded all Jews in every generation to celebrate the Passover festival *for ever* (KJV). It was to remind them and their children of their miraculous liberation and rescue from Egypt. God has never changed this rule.

For thousands of years, the Passover, or Pesach, has been faithfully commemorated; in remembrance of the time when the destroyer *passed over* the homes of those who had smeared their doorposts with the blood of a lamb.

The people have regularly eaten the prescribed bitter herbs (Ex 12:8) in memory of the bitter oppression their forefathers suffered in Egypt. The special meal also consists of Matza, an unleavened bread, for the people left Egypt in such haste that their dough had no time to rise before baking (Ex 12:34).

God clearly commanded that these rules for eating the Passover Lamb were not given for one specific day only. Every year, at the same time, they were to celebrate that unforgettable occasion. Why? Because that was the night they became a nation! That night God came to their rescue! That night Israel stepped into her calling!

No wonder Jews in every age have kept Pesach to their Lord, and have celebrated it by eating the Passover Lamb. Although the Nazis were fine-combing the shell-shattered ruins of the Warsaw ghetto, threatening the lives of any remaining Jews, the faithful still celebrated Pesach during Passover week (Easter week). *Obey these instructions as a lasting ordinance for you and your descendants* (Ex 12:24).

So the children of Israel left Egypt, and eventually reached Sinai. There the Lord said to them: *Now if you obey me fully and keep my covenant, then out of all nations you will be my treasured possession. Although the whole earth is mine, you will be for me a kingdom of priests and a holy nation* (Ex 19:5-6).

A Separate People

At Sinai, God revealed His plan for Israel as a nation and the reason they were to be His "chosen people". As His treasured possession they were to become a kingdom of priests, an entire nation of holy people. God wanted a people distinct and separate from others; a people who would keep His commands and devote themselves to Him.

God wanted a consecrated and holy people—a people separated for service to Him. He wanted a people who would be open to receive and guard the holy revelation He was about to entrust to them.

They were to shine like a light to the rest of the nations—the Gentile world. His people were to teach other peoples the ways of the Lord, both by word and by example.

God's calling to Israel was that they should consecrate themselves and be separate. They were not to imitate the heathen nations around them. The Gentiles (that is, the Goyim, or non-Jewish peoples) had their own customs, laws, religions and idols that were displeasing to God. Their morals, manners, religions and subcultures were hateful to Him (Rom 1:18-32; Gen 6:5-6, 8:21).

God wanted a people who would be His friends; who would respect Him, love and serve Him, the One True God, the Living God, El Shaddai. If this people would accept His word, God could spread His blessing through them to every nation on earth.

God's promise to Abraham had been, *All peoples on earth will be blessed through you* (Gen 12:3). This promise was given to Isaac in Genesis 26:4, *Through your offspring all nations on earth will be blessed.* In the light of this, consider Jesus' words: *Salvation is from the Jews* (John 4:22).

There in the Sinai desert, at the foot of Mount Horeb, God declared His laws to the children of Israel. *He has revealed his word to Jacob, his laws and decrees to Israel. He has done this for no other nation; they do not know his laws* (Ps 147:19-20).

It is important to understand God's purposes here. In order to reach *all* nations He chose *one* of them. As that nation progressed through history, it would reveal God's plans for all creation.

At this point we can look at the prophet Balaam, who was called by Balak, king of Moab, to curse the children of Israel and stop them from entering their promised land. The Spirit of the Lord came over Balaam, however, and instead of cursing them, he pronounced a blessing on them. In the light of God's plan for choosing Israel, notice what he prophesied that others would say about this chosen nation.

> How shall I curse, whom God has not cursed? And how shall I denounce whom the Lord has not denounced? For from the top of the rocks I see him, And from the hills I behold him; There! A people dwelling alone, Not reckoning itself among the nations (Num 23:8-9, NKJV).

> No misfortune is seen in Jacob, no misery observed in Israel. The Lord their God is with them; the shout of the King is among them. God brought them out of Egypt; they have the strength of a wild ox. There is no sorcery against Jacob, no divination against Israel. It will now be said of Jacob and of Israel, See what God has done! (Num 23:21-23).

What does all this really mean? It means that God is with the children of Israel. It means that they are separated for Him, distinct from all other peoples. Why? So that the purposes of God in His creation can be realized! The children of Israel, the Jews, play a significant role in God's total plan for all mankind.

The People of the Law

In Sinai, the Lord revealed His plan to Israel and gave them His laws and statutes. First, He gave them the Ten Commandments, engraving them with His own finger into two stone tablets. Then He gave them several laws, regulations and ordinances.

These rules included everything from moral laws concerning relationships, to the directions for setting up the tabernacle and the rules governing service in it, rules that would later be used in the temple. There were ordinances for the festivals, regulations listing what was holy and unholy, clean and unclean, and rules about eating and drinking.

To the non-Jew living thousands of years later, these precepts can seem unnecessary and irrelevant. As a non-Jew, it is easy to see them as outdated dictates, and not applicable to us who are free from the law. But such a view leads to a superficial reading of the Bible, missing the historical context and purpose of these laws.

The Ten Commandments are still in effect today. If we are free from the law, are we free to steal, lie, murder, or commit adultery? Of course not!

Secondly, these laws, rules and ordinances were given to God's people, to regulate their relationships to Him and to one another, when they came into the land He had promised them. Why? Because God wanted to train up a nation in holiness and righteousness. He wanted a nation who would practice His presence in the midst of a heathen world. This is why He told them they were to keep His laws *for ever.*

A non-Jew can easily miss the fact that God has chosen the nation of Israel forever. It is easy for him to forget that the promises, covenants and rules God gave Israel are *for ever.*

Pesach was to be celebrated *for ever* and so were the other festivals, Shavuot (Pentecost or Whitsun) and Succoth (Feast of Tabernacles). The same is true of the Sabbath (Ex 31:16-17) and circumcision (Gen 17:9-14), which were to be observed *for the generations to come.* God's clear commands are given in the Law for the observation of these feasts.

It is interesting to note that when Paul spoke of the function of the Law, and its implication to the Jew and Gentile, he said, *The law is holy, and the commandment is holy, righteous and good* (Rom 7:12). Many non-Jews perceive the Law to be negative and inappropriate for our society today. However, such an idea is unbiblical and obviously non-Jewish.

The Jew regards the Law (Torah) as God's word and the very expression of Himself. The children of Israel are the people of the Law, the ones to whom it was given. Listen to the psalmist:

> Praise be to you, O Lord; teach me your *decrees.* With my lips I recount all the *laws* that come from your mouth. I rejoice in following your *statutes* as one rejoices in great riches. I meditate in your *precepts* and consider your *ways.* I delight in your *decrees;* I will not neglect your *word.* Do good to your servant, and I will live; I will obey your *word.* Open my eyes that I may see wonderful things in your *law.* I am a stranger on earth; do not hide your *commands* from me (Ps 119:12-19).

God wanted His people to respect His Law and obey it, as the expression of His will and of His holiness. Jesus himself said:

> Do not think that I have come to abolish the Law or the Prophets; I have not come to abolish them but to fulfill them. I tell you the truth, until heaven and earth disappear, not the smallest letter, not the least stroke of a pen, will by any means disappear from the Law until everything is accomplished (Matt 5:17-18).

The children of Israel then became the people of the Law. They held it in the highest esteem, and copied every letter in the most minute detail, so that nothing would be altered or spoiled. They have upheld and defended the Law throughout the centuries.

During the Second World War, Rabbis and other Jews were ready to sacrifice their lives as the Nazis wrecked their synagogues and burned or tore their Torah parchment scrolls into shreds. As the orthodox Jews clung to their treasured Scriptures, the Law of God, vainly trying to shield them from desecration, they were often subjected to public jeering. Some were even kicked to death in their valiant attempt to save the scrolls from what they imagined to be Christian SS soldiers.

Blessing or Curse?

Through the Law, given by God at Sinai, the Israelites entered into their identity as the people of God. They received His everlasting covenant with them. They received His promises and the duties they were to fulfill in return. The commands, the blessings and the curses were all included in the covenant-contract between God and His people.

No other nation had ever been given this privilege. Why? Because God had chosen them and called them through the faith of their forefathers. God had set His heart on His people who were vital to His plans for the whole of mankind. The Lord is continually heard to say: *You will be my people, and I will be your God* (Jer 30:22).

As God confirmed His covenant with His people through the Law at Sinai, He also reaffirmed the promises He had given to the patriarchs, Abraham, Isaac and Jacob. Then, through Moses, came the conditions for the fulfillment of these promises.

From now on, because the people responded positively to God's offer and conditions, they automatically became an obedient (or disobedient) people. They had accepted God's covenant by saying, *We will do everything the Lord has said; we will obey* (Ex 24:7).

Obedience to God and His Law brings blessing. Disobedience brings a curse. *If you fully obey the Lord your God and carefully follow all his commands I give you today, the Lord your God will set you high above all the nations on earth. All these blessings will come upon you and accompany you if you obey the Lord your God* (Deut 28:1-2).

However, if you do not obey the Lord your God and do not carefully follow all his commands and decrees I am giving you today, all these curses will come upon you and overtake you (Deut 28:15).

These verses have caused some to regard God as being capricious and easily irritated. They have talked about God in the Old Testament as the God of wrath, and God in the New Testament as the God of love. However, this is not true, and it is theologically incorrect.

God is unchanging in His nature and consistent in His actions. He is revealed as loving in the Old Testament too. In Jeremiah 31:3 He says to Israel, *I have loved you with an everlasting love; I have drawn you with loving-kindness.*

So when we read in Deuteronomy 28 of the blessing and the curse, it is, in fact, an offer from God to bless Israel. Under the umbrella of the covenant there is protection and blessing, but outside, the same conditions that have applied to the rest of fallen creation since Eden, are operative.

Through the Fall, mankind has experienced sin, sickness, hatred, war, loneliness, poverty and death. Only by virtue of God's covenant of grace, of His generous restoration and blessing, can a person know anything other than the curse that sin brings. God forces His blessing upon no one. However, it may be received and enjoyed by a person's deliberate decision to keep the duties of the covenant.

This is why the Lord says through Moses, in Deuteronomy 30:19-20:

> This day I call heaven and earth as witnesses against you that I have set before you life and death, blessings and curses. Now *choose life*, so that you and your children may live and that you may love the Lord your God, listen to his voice, and hold fast to him. For the Lord is your life, and he will give you many years in the land he swore to give to your fathers, Abraham, Isaac and Jacob.

The Calling

As the children of Israel left Sinai, the whole of their future was mapped out. God's plan for them was blessing, growth, possession of the land, and a life of abundance and true worship of Him there.

In this way, God would be able to increasingly reveal Himself to them, and so prepare His people for the coming Messiah. The glory of the Lord would fill the earth, Israel would become a light to the nations, law and order would proceed from Zion and the kingdom of the Messiah would come.

Such was God's plan, which He revealed with increasing clarity through the prophets. We must understand that Bible revelation is progressive. More and more are added to the puzzle until the final picture can be seen.

Thus, Israel is to become both God's model and His showpiece, situated centrally among the nations. In return, all He asks of them is to *Love the Lord your God with all your heart and with all your soul and with all your strength* (Deut 6:5).

While the whole of the Old Testament is a progressive revelation of God's will for His people (and for all other peoples, as well), it is also the story of Israel's struggle to obey Him amid many temptations. It describes both God's miraculous power to save, restore, protect and bless them, and the unhappy consequences of their backsliding and disobedience.

It is easy for an outsider to read the Bible's honest account and then criticize Israel for her decisions. Why didn't the people listen more closely to Moses? Why wasn't Gideon thanked for his efforts? Why did Solomon, who had everything he ever want, fall? Why were Elisha, Jeremiah and the other prophets persecuted?

However, before we criticize, we ought to put ourselves in their situation. It is easy to be wise after the event.

And where else in world history do we find a nation so openly and nakedly recounting its lacks, mistakes and shortcomings? National histories almost invariably smack of self-justification, self-commendation, excuses, whitewashing and revaluations.

Here, in contrast, we have a people with a solemn, yet gloriously unique calling. It is a calling that affects the future of not only every nation and person on earth, but creation itself. Therefore, it is not surprising that there should be such a colossal battle over Israel. This is the battle depicted in the Bible.

The Curse: Consequence of Disobedience

God warned His people, Israel, what would happen if they misused His blessings or lost their faith in Him. He told them through Moses, *The Lord will scatter you among all nations, from one end of the earth to the other* (Deut 28:64). Despite His warning, however, we read throughout the Old Testament that Israel repeatedly fell away from God.

The Lord sent them judges, prophets, priests and kings to rescue them, admonish them and restore them. But there was constant pressure in each successive generation from other countries, other cultures and other gods. They were constantly tempted to compromise, modify or assimilate themselves.

When they faced adverse circumstances in the desert the people cried to Moses, Let's go back to Egypt! When they were without a king, they called out to Samuel, *Now appoint a king to lead us, such as all the other nations have* (1 Sam 8:5).

When, because of sin, the people came under the heel of other nations (the Midianites, the Ammonites and the Philistines), they would call out to the Lord, and He would send them rescuers (Judg 6:1-16). However, they soon fell away, beginning with compromise and finishing up, once more, under heathen influence from the surrounding nations.

Heathen cults and idolatry, demon worship and the occult were introduced through kings like Jeroboam, Ahab and others, although the Law expressly prohibited them. Queen Jezebel supported hundreds of prophets of Baal. She planted gardens for idol worship and burned children in sacrifice to the god, Moloch, in the Valley of Hinnom. Things went so far that idols were even set up in the Temple courtyard, and the Book of the Law was lost.

However, the reign of King Josiah brought a period of reformation (2 Kings 22). The Temple was rebuilt and its services reinstated. During this restoration process, the Law book was found hidden in a dusty corner, where it had been lying unused for years.

Hilkiah, the high priest, took it to the king and began to read it aloud. On hearing it, King Josiah was terrified and tore his royal robes, realizing that his people had broken the law and come under its curse. They were unrighteous! They must repent! Through the consequent revival, the king diverted God's anger from His people.

A further example of renewal and reformation can be seen in the days of King Hezekiah. *He held fast to the Lord and did not cease to follow him; he kept the commands the Lord had given Moses.... He removed the high places, smashed the sacred stones and cut down the Asherah poles* (2 Kings 18:6,4).

Because of this, the Lord was with him in all that he did and blessed him.

The Role of the Prophets

Whenever Israel turned away from God and His law, He sent prophets to correct them and lead them back. Isaiah, Jeremiah, Hosea, Amos and the other prophets all had the same task. They pronounced judgments against ungodliness and unjust actions but they also spoke of grace, forgiveness, restoration and blessing as well.

No prophet ever said, All right, that's it! That was your last chance. You're finished as a people and a nation. Every prophet who pronounced judgment also spoke of restoration. When the prophets spoke of scattering, they also talked of regathering.

At length, though, God let judgment fall upon the people of Israel. He uprooted them from their land and sentenced them to seventy years' captivity in Babylon. Thus, Jeremiah laments:

> The roads to Zion mourn, for no one comes to her appointed feasts. All her gateways are desolate, her priests groan, her maidens grieve, and she is in bitter anguish. Her foes have become her masters; her enemies are at ease. The Lord has brought her grief because of her many sins. Her children have gone into exile, captive before the foe. All the splendor has departed from the Daughter of Zion (Lam 1:4-6).

What a plight! All hopes of what God had promised were shattered. The temple was burned to the ground, the city walls were demolished and Jerusalem lay in ruins. God, who had once been her shield and protection, her fortress and her stronghold, was now very distant. Instead of coming with grace, God came with judgment.

Hosea 4:1 says, *The Lord has a charge to bring against you who live in the land: There is no faithfulness, no love, no acknowledgment of God in the land.*

Isaiah 1:4,7 continues, *Ah, sinful nation, a people loaded with guilt, a brood of evildoers, children given to corruption. They have forsaken the Lord; they have spurned the Holy One of Israel and turned their backs on him.... Your country is desolate, your cities burned with fire; your fields are being stripped by foreigners right before you, laid waste as when overthrown by strangers.*

What a disaster! Everything Moses had spoken, all that God had promised and imparted at Sinai, all that David had sung about and Solomon had built, was gone. Nothing was left. The land was destroyed. Jerusalem was burned down and the people were led away into captivity. Where were the promises now? Hope was gone. Discouragement, disappointment, sorrow and wretchedness were all that remained.

No doubt many wondered, Has God left us forever? Are we rejected from His presence? The words of the prophets had been fulfilled. They had issued their warnings, but the people had not listened, and now they felt wretched. Will the land fall to others? Will our nation die out like so many others have?

The Faithfulness of God

Then God spoke:

> This is what the Lord says, he who appoints the sun to shine by day, who decrees the moon and stars to shine by night, who stirs up the sea so that its waves roar the Lord Almighty is his name: Only if these decrees vanish from my sight, declares the Lord, will the descendants of Israel ever cease to be a nation before me (Jer 31:35-36).

God has no plans for the dissolution of His people! *I myself will gather the remnant of my flock out of all the countries where I have driven them...* (Jer 23:3). This is exactly what He had promised Moses He would do if, after the people had backslided, they returned to Him: *The Lord your God will restore your fortunes and have compassion on you and gather you again from all the nations where he scattered you* (Deut 30:3).

Not one prophet condemned the people forever. Every sin can be forgiven, every transgression atoned for. After every judgment, there is a restoration, and after every scattering, a regathering.

Why? Because the children of Israel are God's chosen people forever. Because the covenant of God is everlasting! Because His promises to their forefathers never fail! This is why He says to the scorched and desolate earth in Ezekiel 36:8, *But you, O mountains of Israel, will produce branches and fruit for my people Israel, for they will soon come home.*

God can never forget His promises. He has not forgotten His plans or His people. He will never forget His land, nor forsake His city—the place to which He has attached His own name. He has said of Jerusalem: *The Lord has chosen Zion, he has desired it for his dwelling; This is my resting place for ever and ever...* (Ps 132:13-14).

When the situation looked darker than ever, the promises shone like a light in a dismal wilderness. God still means what He said about His people! His aims will always be realized and his people will be blessed. His promises are forever!

2

The Land

Lift up your eyes from where you are and look north and south, east and west. All that you see I will give to you and your offspring forever (Gen 13:14-15).

The God of History

It is impossible to understand modern Israel and the Jewish people, without carefully considering the calling God has given them. Current Middle East affairs are equally inexplicable without background knowledge of the Bible narrative. God's word and His calling are crucial, if we are to comprehend fully events in and around Israel at this time.

God is totally involved in history because He deals with people, places and facts. Other religions ignore facts, focusing instead on fable and fantasy. But the God of Israel is the Truth and He deals in realities. Therefore, He is inextricably involved with people and situations. There is nothing abstract about God, unlike many philosophies. He will use a land and a people to bless the whole of mankind. Without the land and without the people, His will and plans cannot be understood.

From the very beginning, God moved to fulfill His plans. After the Fall, God restored His severed fellowship with mankind, by selecting one man to become the forefather of a people. This would be the nation through whom the Messiah would be born and the Messiah would in turn, bring blessing to all mankind. As early as Genesis 3:15, we find God saying to the serpent, *I will put enmity between you and the woman, and between your offspring and hers; he will crush your head and you will strike his heel*. Even at the dawn of history, God was already implementing His plan and promising mankind that someone would come to break Satan's dominion and reestablish fellowship with Himself. But how would it be done? And when?

Several generations passed and the human race increased and spread throughout the earth. However, as man increased, so too, did sin.

We read in Genesis 6:5-6:

> The Lord saw how great man's wickedness on the earth had become, and that every inclination of the thoughts of his heart was evil all the time. The Lord was grieved that he had made man on the earth, and his heart was filled with pain.

Sin multiplied and judgment followed, bringing the Flood. Afterwards, God began all over again, with Noah. He and his three sons, Shem, Ham and Japheth, became the new forefathers of all the subsequent inhabitants of the earth.

Through the line of Shem, a man called Eber was born (Gen 11:14). (The word Hebrew is believed to have come from his name.) Then many years later, Nahor was born. He became the father of Terah, and Terah the father of Abram.

The Promise of the Land

Abram lived in Ur in Chaldea, today's Iraq. God called him out of Ur and at this point, God's plan of salvation moved forward dramatically. Instead of working generally with every nation, He chose one nation through whom He intended to bless *all* the others. The purpose in His heart remained the same; only His methods and ways changed.

The Lord had said to Abram, *Leave your country, your people and your father's household and go to the land I will show you. I will make you into a great nation and I will bless you; I will make your name great, and you will be a blessing. I will bless those who bless you, and whoever curses you I will curse; and all peoples on earth will be blessed through you* (Gen 12:1-3).

God had now chosen a man, Abram, through whom He intended to bless the whole of mankind. In order for this to happen, God promised him two things: He promised Abram a land and He promised him that he would become a people.

When Abram obeyed and arrived at the land of Canaan, God said to him: *To your offspring I will give this land* (Gen 12:7). This meant that Abram's descendants would receive a land they could call their own. Later, after Lot left Abram because of quarrels between their herdsmen, the Lord came to Abram again and told him:

> Lift up your eyes from where you are and look north and south, east and west. All the land that you see I will give to you and your offspring forever. I will make your offspring like the dust of the earth, so that if anyone could count the dust, then your offspring could be counted. Go, walk through the length and breadth of the land, for I am giving it to you (Gen 13:14-17).

From every place where Abram stood, as far as he could see in every direction, lay the land that God was promising him. But for how long was the promise to be in effect? Verse 15 has our answer—Forever.

This means that God's promise to Abram and to his descendants, to live in the land of Israel, was not limited to one or just a few generations. The promise was to belong to the descendants of Abram, forever.

The Covenant with Abraham

As Abram continued to walk with God in Canaan, so God revealed His plans to him. God told Abram that he would receive a son and become a populous nation. He reaffirmed to Abram that the land belonged to him.

I am the Lord, God told him, who brought you out of Ur of the Chaldeans to give you this land to take possession of it (Gen 15:7).

Abram responded by asking, *O Sovereign Lord, how can I know that I will gain possession of it?* (Gen 15:8).

God answered Abram by entering a covenant with him. That covenant was sealed by means of a smoking fire pot and a blazing torch passing between the carcasses of the animals, which Abram had been ordered to divide (Gen 15:9-17). God declared to him, *To your descendants I give this land, from the river of Egypt, to the great river, the Euphrates* (Gen 15:18).

He carefully repeated His promise of the land to Abram over and over again. God expressly entered an everlasting covenant with Abram, to reassure him that the land would belong to his descendants, forever. The borders and the extent of the land are mentioned for the first time in this covenant.

Later, God changed Abram's name to Abraham, and entered further covenants with him. In Genesis 17, God said to Abraham, I have made you a father of many nations (v. 5). He declared again that the covenant was everlasting (v. 7), adding in verse 8, *The whole land of Canaan, where you are now an alien, I will give as an everlasting possession to you and your descendants after you; and I will be their God.* The external token of this covenant was circumcision.

God's promises to Abraham were as follows:

1. God had entered an everlasting covenant with him (Gen 17:7).

2. Abraham would be the father of many nations (Gen 17:4-5).

3. He would be the father of the children of Israel. Blessings would come upon many peoples, but God established His covenant with Isaac (Gen 17:19-21). The chosen people of God would come through Isaac.

4. Abraham's people would receive a land forever (Gen 17:8).

5. The people would know and serve the Lord and He would be their God (Gen 17:7-8).

The foundation was now laid and the covenant established: God had spoken and revealed His will. The revelation of God Himself and His will was established because of this covenant with Abraham, and it was enlarged throughout successive generations. God continued to perform miracles and mighty acts so that His will would be done and the whole of mankind could enter His blessing (Gen 12:3, 22:18).

The covenant was renewed with Isaac and God promised him:

Stay in this land for a while, and I will be with you and will bless you. For to you and your descendants I will give all these lands and will confirm the oath I swore to your father Abraham. I will make your descendants as numerous as the stars in the sky and will give them all these lands, and through your offspring all nations on earth will be blessed (Gen 26:3-4).

Isaac became the father of two sons, Esau and Jacob. However, instead of the covenant promise passing on to Esau, the elder son, it was given to Jacob. Like his grandfather, Abraham, Jacob also received a new name from God; he would be called Israel (Gen 32:28).

In the Land

Jacob experienced a long, arduous journey until he encountered God and his life was changed. It began with a conflict. Jacob cheated his brother Esau out of his father's blessing. Then, because of Esau's anger, Jacob was forced to flee the land.

However, when he returned many years later, God blessed him. As he reentered the land, he retraced the route his forefather Abraham had taken. First, he went to Shechem and then to Bethel. At Bethel, he built an altar and there God revealed Himself to Jacob and told him several things:

1. *Your name will be Israel* (Gen 35:10).

2. *A community of nations will come from you* (Gen 35:11).

3. *The land I gave to Abraham and Isaac I also give to you, and I will give this land to your descendants after you* (Gen 35:12).

As God confirmed the covenant with Jacob, we see again that God constantly renewed His promise of the land. He is the God of Abraham, Isaac and Jacob; the God who gave them the land as an everlasting possession.

Jacob's twelve sons would become the twelve tribes of Israel. On his deathbed, he prophesied over each of them, speaking about the future nation, the land and the coming Messiah (Gen 49).

At this stage, the people were still living in Egypt, just as the Lord had predicted to Abraham (Gen 15:13). They had increased, but also suffered terrible oppression until God spoke to Moses and told him to liberate His people. Their freedom eventually came and after eating unleavened bread and the Passover lamb, they boldly departed. God then performed tremendous miracles to save them.

Having saved them, God spoke to them again. At Mount Horeb in Sinai, He showed Himself to them and gave them the Ten Commandments, the Law and the rules of service for the tabernacle. As God delivered the commandments to them, He again repeated his promise of the land. *Honor your father and your mother, so that you may live long* **in the land** *the Lord your God is giving you* (Ex 20:12).

The whole point of Israel's liberation from Egypt was to come to the Promised Land. God's purpose in giving all the rules and regulations at Sinai was that they should be kept in the land. The entire plan of the tabernacle was a foreshadowing of the temple that was to come. It showed the work to be done there, and the festivals and sacrifices that the Lord wanted when they came to live *in the land.*

The Covenant is Valid Today

The promises God gave to the patriarchs, Abraham, Isaac and Jacob, were thus passed on as an inheritance to the twelve tribes—the whole nation of Israel. From the time of their exodus from Egypt, the people were reckoned as a nation. They had the

Law (Torah) and were on their way to their own land, Eretz Israel. Psalm 105:6-11 says:

> O descendants of Abraham his servant, O sons of Jacob, his chosen ones. He is the Lord our God; his judgments are in all the earth. He remembers his covenant forever, the word he commanded, *for a thousand generations,* the covenant he made with Abraham, the oath he swore to Isaac. He confirmed it to Jacob as a decree, to Israel as an everlasting covenant: *To you I will give the land of Canaan* as the portion you will inherit.

It cannot be stated more plainly! The Almighty said it to Abraham, He said it to Isaac, He said it to Jacob and He said it to Israel. The promise was declared under oath when God made the everlasting covenant with His people.

God continually has the covenant in mind. He said that it was valid for a thousand generations. A thousand generations has not passed since God spoke to Abraham, so what God said is still in effect today. This land, with the boundaries He described, is an area of land reserved for the children of Israel.

As we consider this, we must first realize that the land is God's, not anyone else's. He created the entire earth, and it is His. Secondly, since He owns it, He can divide it up as He wills. He has given a small part of this earth to His chosen people so that they may live there and serve Him, and from there be a blessing to the whole earth.

Three Key Places:
Hebron, Shechem, Jerusalem

If we are not familiar with this historical background, it is impossible to understand what is happening in

Israel and the rest of the Middle East today. God had spoken to the patriarchs and given the land to the children of Israel, forever.

God is exact in everything He does, and everything He does is legally righteous. Today, there are many complaints against modern Israel, implying that the country exists because they have stolen the land from the Arabs. This is not true. However, to understand the situation properly, we must be clear about the historical background.

When God spoke to Abraham, he was still a stranger in the land of Canaan. This is emphasized when we read of Abraham's arrangements to bury Sarah, his wife. In Genesis 23:12-18 we learn that he spoke to the Hittites in Hebron about buying the cave in Machpelah, at the end of Ephron's field. Ephron sold it to him for 400 shekels of silver. In this proper and legally correct way, Abraham became the rightful owner of a tract of land in Hebron.

> So Ephron's field in Machpelah near Mamre both the field and the cave in it, and all the trees within the borders of the field was deeded to Abraham as his property in the presence of all the Hittites who had come to the gate of the city (Gen 23:17-18).

Years later, when Joshua had possessed the land, *Joseph's bones, which the Israelites had brought up from Egypt, were buried in Shechem in the tract of land that Jacob bought for a hundred pieces of silver from the sons of Hamor, the father of Shechem* (Josh 24:32).

Later still, we read in Second Samuel 24:15-25 how King David bought the threshing floor from Ornan (Araunah) for 50 shekels of silver. This is the same place as Mount Moriah, where Isaac was to have been sacrificed, and also the site of the future temple.

All three of these places, Hebron, Shechem and Mount Moriah, were visited by Abraham. All three were also vital to God's plans for the children of Israel. Shechem was the place of the covenant in the land (see Deut 11:29-30; Josh 8:30-35), Hebron was David's capital before he chose Jerusalem, and Mount Moriah was the site of the temple.

When Arabs today oppose Israel's presence in the Middle East and demand the return of the so-called West Bank (which is really Israel's heartland, Judea and Samaria), Arab resistance is fiercest from Nablus (Shechem), Hebron and the Temple Mount in East Jerusalem.

The Word of God promises the entire country to Abraham's descendants, the Israelis. Moreover, it is precisely these three places that were bought and paid for by Abraham, Jacob and David. Surely, these sites, if any, belong to Israel.

The purchases have never been canceled. Land that is legally bought does not fall to another just because the owner leaves it for a time, while on a journey. It is significant that Ezekiel prophesies:

> The enemy said of you, Aha! The ancient heights have become our possession. Therefore prophesy and say, This is what the Sovereign Lord says: Because they ravaged and hounded you from every side so that you became the possession of the rest of the nations and the object of people's malicious talk and slander, Therefore, O mountains of Israel, hear the word of the Sovereign Lord: This is what the Sovereign Lord says to the mountains and hills, to the ravines and valleys, to the desolate ruins and the deserted towns that have been plundered and ridiculed by the rest of the nations around you (Ezek 36:2-4).

The Desert is Blossoming!

This is precisely what has happened. These sites, obtained by both legal purchase and divine gift, lie on the so-called West Bank today. And from here comes the main resistance to the presence of the Jews in their own land. But neither the so-called West Bank, Arab opposition, nor plans for an Arabic Palestine can annul the fact that God has given the land to the children of Israel.

Israel has been accused of stealing the land from the Arabs, but such complaints falsify historical facts. When Jewish Zionists began to return to Zion at the end of the 1800's, very few Arabs lived in the country. It had fallen into the hands of rich Arab landowners living in Turkey, Damascus and Cairo.

The land was largely unfit for farming, and it was this almost worthless earth that the Jewish pioneers had to buy at high prices. No one thought anyone would want it, believing it could not be farmed profitably. But when the Jews bought it, drained it and transformed it into arable land, the situation suddenly changed.

The Arabs counteracted and began to match the immigration of the Jews with their own. Arabs began moving in from the opposite direction, to stem the tide of Jewish immigration. Later, after Israel's independence in 1948 and the ensuing war of liberation, refugee problems arose. Arabs, who had settled there as little as *two years* earlier, were recognized as refugees.

In other words, many Arabs had scarcely moved in. They had not lived in the land for hundreds of years, as one can easily be led to believe.

Today, there is widespread discussion of the refugee problem and, of course, Israel is also discussed. Many put forward their reasons about whether the Jews should or should not be allowed to live in the land. Some give historical reasons, others give humanitarian reasons. Some point to the holocaust, and others to the UN decision of 1947. The arguments are various and many.

However, over and above these various opinions lies the deciding factor: God has given the land to the Jews. The testimony of Scripture is unequivocal, God has said it is theirs *for ever.*

3

The Curse of Anti-Semitism

In the very first book of the Bible, we encounter the origin of anti-Semitism that can be traced throughout Church history to the present day. Anti-Semitism has assumed different names and aligned itself with differing ideologies, religious as well as secular. However, it has always had the same target—the liberty of the Jewish people, their security and their very existence.

Genesis 3:15 provides the source of this enmity, as God told Satan that the woman's seed, or offspring, would crush the serpent's head. God would use the woman's seed to take back all that Satan had stolen through the Fall.

God's plan was that the Seed of the woman would come through Abraham. Abraham's seed is the children of Israel. It was through them the Messiah would come and through them, too, that God would bless mankind. They were to be a different people and love God with all their heart.

We should not be surprised, then, that this sin-stricken world, full of idolatry, selfishness and hostility toward God, became a breeding ground for hatred toward the people He had chosen. Rooted in envy and hatred, anti-Semitism has made its presence known from earliest times.

Even Isaac, Abraham's son, met it. Genesis 26:14 and 27 tells us about the reaction of Abimelech's people toward him.

He had so many flocks and herds and servants that the Philistines envied him.... Isaac asked them, Why have you come to me, since you were hostile to me and sent me away?

The Presence of God's People unmasks Spirit Powers

Another example of anti-Semitism was encountered by the children of Israel, while they were still in Egypt. As they had increased, so too had the hatred against them. Then, as they reached the threshold of becoming a nation, plans to annihilate them took shape. They were oppressed, forced into slavery, afflicted with inhuman slave labor and their newborn sons were killed.

Eventually, the Lord delivered them from their tormentors, but the evil, spirit power that had persecuted them did not give up. Hatred, threats and intimidation met them from every direction. Other nations saw them as a danger. Rahab told the spies who hid in her house in Jericho, *a great fear of you has fallen on us, so that all who live in this country are melting in fear because of you* (Josh 2:9).

The surrounding nations felt either respect and affection, or envy and hatred toward Israel; depending on the level of their relationship with Israel's God. Her presence revealed what was in the heart of the peoples: Love or hate, rebellion or faith toward the Lord, the God of Israel.

When Israel was strong in her Lord, she rose above the resistance she met; when she was weak, she succumbed. However, the phenomena never ceased. It was always present, because an evil spirit power lay behind it all. It was a demonically inspired hatred and revolt against God's plan for the restoration of mankind.

The enemy has always tried to hinder or wipe out the Jewish nation, in an attempt to stop the prophecies of God from being fulfilled.

After the captivity in Babylon, when the Lord called His people back to Zion, yet another demonic plan began to hatch. Haman the Agagite suddenly had the idea of exterminating all the Jews. The book of Esther recounts the story of Haman's fury, when Mordecai refused to bow the knee to him.

Haman's fury, however, was not only directed at Mordecai, but at his entire nation. Haman said to the king:

> There is a certain people dispersed and scattered among the peoples in all the provinces of your kingdom who keep themselves separate. Their customs are different from those of all other people, and they do not obey the king's laws; it is not in the king's best interest to tolerate them.... If it pleases the king, let a decree be issued to destroy them and I will put ten thousand talents into the royal treasury for the men who carry out this business (Esth 3:8-9).

This scripture encapsulates the Jews' problem. Such is the face of anti-Semitism.

When Mordecai refused to bow, anti-Semitism reared its head in the typical way. Haman accused the Jews of three things:

1. There is a certain people dispersed and scattered among the peoples—implying that they were infiltrators,

2. Whose customs are different from those of all other people—implying they are different, and

3. Who do not obey the king's laws—intimating that they were neither law-abiding nor loyal, but disloyal and not to be trusted (Esth 3:8).

A study of anti-Semitism's long and tragic history reveals the perpetual repetition of such accusations.

On another occasion, Shadrach, Meshach and Abednego suffered a similar fate when they refused to fall down to the false gods and idols of Babylon. It was said of them:

> There are some Jews whom you have set over the affairs of the province of Babylon—Shadrach, Meshach and Abednego—who pay no attention to you, O King. They neither serve your gods nor worship the image of gold you have set up (Dan 3:12).

No Security in the Dispersion

After their captivity in Babylon, not all the Jews returned home. Many remained. They traveled around, becoming merchants and settling in commercial cities in neighboring countries. After a time, Jewish enclaves and synagogues sprang up all around the Mediterranean Sea. It was these that Paul always visited first when he preached the Gospel, ...*first for the Jew, then for the Gentile* (Rom 1:16).

Hence, we have the dispersion of the Jews, the diaspora. Whenever they settled, it was always more or less by grace, according to the inclination of the kings or rulers of these communities. The Jews mainly reacted in two different ways toward this situation: Some took an orthodox religious stance, while others favored assimilation.

The latter did all they could to be like everyone around them. They changed their lifestyle and became enterprising and loyal citizens in the lands where they lived. Such Jews were absorbed into the current religion and culture.

Others clung firmly to the faith of their fathers, despite their environment. Daniel provides such an example. When the decree, prohibiting worship of anyone other than King Darius, was issued, he continued as before to pray to his God, three times a day.

> Now when Daniel learned that the decree had been published, he went to his upstairs room where the windows opened toward Jerusalem. Three times a day, he got down on his knees and prayed, giving thanks to his God, just as he had done before (Dan 6:10).

Daniel neither changed his lifestyle, nor gave in to the anti-Semitism of his day.

Everyone's Scapegoat

Anti-Semitism can be Persian, Greek or Roman. It can be Muslim, Nazi, religious, worldly or Christian. But it invariably contains the same three indictments: They're different, they're a threat and they're disloyal conspirators who can't be trusted.

When Moses prophesied the dispersion, he said:

> Then the Lord will scatter you among all nations, from one end of the earth to the other. There you will worship other gods—gods of wood and stone, which neither you nor your fathers have known. Among those other nations you will find no repose, no resting place for the sole of your foot. There the Lord will give you an anxious mind, eyes weary with longing, and a despairing heart. You will live in constant suspense, filled with dread both night and day, never sure of your life (Deut 28:64-66).

Moses' prophecy has indeed come to pass. How many of us have not been either hostile, spiteful, scheming or at least envious toward this race? Even in times of security, their situation has abruptly changed as new waves of persecution have rolled over them.

In generation after generation, the same evil spirit power has reared its head with its unswerving aim—to humiliate, obstruct, persecute and, if possible, exterminate the Jews. Its intention has always been the same, only the methods have changed.

During the time of Ezra and Nehemiah, many Jews returned home to their land. However, Gentile political powers always held sway in the country, bringing their heathen customs and rites with them. The Romans and Greeks set up their holds and defiled the land with their outlandish habits. Sorrow must have filled the hearts of faithful Jews to see their land and people, whom God has separated for Himself, under heathen influence.

Furthermore, the occupying power often provoked the Jews when they committed deeds prohibited in the Law of God. It was demeaning, too, for the High Priests to have to ask permission from their Roman overlords, before using the priestly robes at the festivals. These robes were kept in the Antonia Fortress by the Romans, and only allowed out on a few occasions. Such situations produce frustration and impatience.

Jewish zealots were knifing Roman soldiers, and the Romans were becoming exceedingly tired of this stubborn people, who refused to pray to Mars and Jupiter and would never enter the house of a non-Jew. Finally, the situation exploded.

FOR MORE INFORMATION
ABOUT PRODUCTS BY
ULF EKMAN
CALL 1-800-428-1760

OR
WRITE TO:
ULF EKMAN MINISTRIES
P.O. BOX 46108
MINNEAPOLIS, MN 55446

Jesus prophesied about it when He wept over the fate of Jerusalem. *They will fall by the sword and will be taken as prisoners to all nations, Jerusalem will be trampled on by the Gentiles until the times of the Gentiles are fulfilled* (Luke 21:24).

The Ninth of Abib

In the year AD 70 the Romans suppressed a Jewish uprising, sacked Jerusalem and burned the temple to the ground. Significantly, it happened on the ninth day of the Jewish month, Abib. The ninth of Abib was a set day of fasting. It was called Tisha Be-Av and was kept for the mourning of the destruction of the first temple.

Hundreds of years earlier, on precisely that day, Nebuchadnezzar had destroyed the first temple. Now, on exactly the same day, the second temple was also destroyed. Remarkably, too, on the same day in 1290, all Jews were banished from England and on that very day in 1492, Jews were expelled from Spain. Several other disasters have befallen the Jewish people on precisely this date.

After killing untold numbers of Jews and scattering even more, the Romans held sway for a time, but in AD 135 another uprising took place. The rabbi, Achiva, pointed out a Messiah, Bar Kochba, who took up the fight against the Romans. Bar Kochba's army was wiped out on the same date, the ninth of Abib, and the Romans drove out the remaining Jews.

Jerusalem was utterly devastated and the place where the temple had once stood was plowed under. On its foundation rose a new city, Aelia Capitolina, into which no Jew was permitted to enter. The final defeat and end of the Jewish people seemed to have come.

The Church is Born

However, at the same time, something entirely new had sprung into being. After Jesus' death and resurrection, came the Day of Pentecost. The Holy Spirit was poured out and the Church was born. It consisted of thousands of Jews who believed that Jesus of Nazareth was the Messiah, and that His death and resurrection was exactly what the prophet had foretold: He was the suffering Servant of the Lord, Messiah Ben-Joseph.*

They believed, too, that He was the one to whom the service in the temple pointed; He was the perfect sacrificial lamb, which was to take away the sin of the people forever. They also believed that at His first coming He was in lowly form. But at His second coming, He would fulfill all the prophecies concerning the house and kingdom of David, as Messiah Ben-David.

As the Church grew, huge numbers of Jews were added to it. They were different in that they went out, as Jesus had commanded them, to the nations, (to the Gentiles). Consequently, many non-Jews began to profess Jesus as the Messiah. The New Testament describes how questions arose in the Jewish Jesus-believing church about whether the

---

* Messiah Ben-Joseph (Joseph's son) referred to Joseph in Egypt as a type of the Messiah in the Old Testament. Even Jewish tradition holds Joseph to be a type of the coming Messiah because of his rejection and exaltation, and because he finally saved his brothers from famine.

Gentile believers were required to keep the Mosaic law or not.

The apostles met to discuss such matters and they found that both the Law and circumcision concerned the Jews only. The Gentile believers should simply abstain from certain kinds of food, such as blood, and from fornication (see Acts 15). This meant that Jews were not to stop practicing circumcision, keeping the Sabbath or celebrating their set festivals, but that the Gentiles need not do so.

Paul described the non-Jewish believers as branches taken from a wild, fruitless olive tree (the heathen nations), and grafted into a cultivated, fruitful olive tree with a nourishing, sap-filled root (Israel). He warned the Gentile believers against boasting and arrogance toward the other branches. Remember, he had said, it is not the branches that support the root, but the root that supports the branches.

If some of the branches have been broken off, and you, though a wild olive shoot, have been grafted in among the others and now share in the nourishing sap from the olive root, do not boast over those branches. If you do, consider this: You do not support the root, but the root supports you (Rom 11:17-18).

The Apostasy of the Church

This was the attitude of the early Church, which was predominantly Jewish. But sadly, Paul's warning was lost on many Gentile believers so that the dreadful phenomenon, Christian anti-Semitism, began to appear. When Greek, non-Jewish believers began to increase and spread throughout the Roman Empire, the believers were called Christians. The name Christian comes from the Greek word for Messiah, Christos.

Among the Christians, the number of non-Jews continually increased. However, this had a negative effect—an increasing estrangement from the root, Israel. As the Christian Church grew, it began to absorb elements that were not only unbiblical but also distinctly and directly anti-Semitic.

By means of various rites, Greek gnosticism secured a foothold in the Church, as did Babylonian mystery cults. Local superstitions, together with struggles for power by certain bishops, also had an effect. Then in the fourth century, the Roman Caesar, Constantine, declared that the struggle against Christianity was lost. He proclaimed religious freedom throughout the Roman Empire and Christianity was declared the official religion.

Many considered this a positive development, but it was, in fact, the opposite. The true Christian revival element subsided, only to be gradually substituted by an authoritarian, church-political institution. This in turn, developed into the Roman Catholic and Greek Orthodox religions we know today. Religion, human traditions, superstitions and legends gained supremacy, while genuine, biblical Christianity gradually disappeared from the scene.

Maryology and veneration of saints came increasingly to the forefront. This development led to a twofold assault: the one, against Bible-based revival movements (which I will not deal with here) and the other, against the Jews. Anti-Semitism on a Christian basis grew even stronger.

To understand this completely, we have to realize what the word Christian means. Christian has become synonymous with several different concepts.

We hear of Christian ethics, Christian culture, the Christian viewpoint, a Christian country, Christian denominations and so forth. In the same way, people talk about Jewish culture, Muslim countries and culture, etc. For the uninitiated, it can sound very confusing.

When a Jew reads about the holocaust under the Nazis, he links it to a country with a Christian culture, to churches and to songs like Silent Night. He imagines Nazis attending church, calling themselves Christians and then joining the mass murder of Jews. Russian Orthodox Christians led pogroms against Jews in this very manner. Examples can be multiplied throughout history.

But were these people Christians? The answer must be both yes and no! Yes, they came from countries with Christian cultures. But were they Christians according to the Bible definition? Never! A person who receives the message of the Gospel is forgiven of his sins and finds peace with God. He is born again, becomes a new creation and is given a new heart.

The Bible tells us that the love of God is poured out in that person's heart. How then can a person like that, who is under command to love all his fellow men, and especially God's chosen people, persecute Jews? Impossible! No true revival Christian can be a persecutor.

A persecutor is someone driven by religious hate, a person who does not know God. Therefore, it is tragic to note that the same religious institutions that have persecuted the Jews, have also persecuted revival Christians.

It is the life in the Holy Spirit, and the promises and covenants of God that have been attacked, persecuted and defamed. Why? Because religion without biblical preaching, conversion and spiritual life is living death. This death hates God's life because it does not have it itself.

Are Christians innocent then? No! The Church has blood on its hands!

Replacement Theology

As the Church inevitably moved away from its Jewish and biblical roots, it accumulated many unbiblical features. As Christianity was proclaimed the official religion of the Roman Empire and its observance became a legal requirement, the Jews were prohibited from holding their festivals.

Replacement Theology, became increasingly prevalent at the time. It asserted that the Church was now the new Israel and that the time of the Jews, as the people of God, was over.

Furthermore, all Jews were condemned to fugitive status, to wander the earth forever as vagabonds or be punished and put to death for murdering Christ. This came not only from the uneducated masses, who were out for excitement or a fight, but also from theologians, from the so-called church fathers, who are venerated for their Christlike example!

In the fifth century, the most renowned preacher of the time, John Chrysostom, uttered these words, among many others: The synagogue is worse than a brothel. The Jews are a bunch of criminals. I hate the synagogue and the Jews *(The Roots of Anti-Semitism,* Malcolm Hay).

Vulgar ideas from similar sermons became popular among ordinary people. Through them, the message was spread that anyone, Christian or non-Christian, who hounded or killed Jews simply executed the wrath of God on them. In other words, it was completely all right.

An extensive list could be made describing how the Jews were persecuted by the Christians: they lost their rights to citizenship; they were denied the right to purchase land or farm it; they were told where to live. Alternatives were out of the question. Jews were expelled from cities and countries. They were outrageously overtaxed and lost their property at the whim of the authorities. They were forcibly baptized and converted. Jews were compelled to march in processions and sing satirical songs about themselves. They were forced to eat pork and to wear special hats and yellow tags on their clothes to make them easily recognizable.

When did this happen? In Germany during the 1930's and 1940's? No, during the whole of Christian church history. Adversity, crop failure and sickness were all blamed on the Jews. The Plague, said the church, is the fault of the Jews. They were accused of poisoning wells and of ritually murdering the children of Christians and using their blood to make unleavened bread.

As a result, Jewish synagogues were burned down. Sometimes, the people were still inside. In Spain, Jews were tortured in the most bestial manner and burnt on funeral pyres.

Ghettos and Pogroms

Those Jews who were forcibly converted, were spied on to see if they were still secretly practicing their religion. Some theologians believed that they should be put to death, saying they are doomed to eternal loss anyhow. Others thought they should be regarded as examples of the awful fate that awaits non-Christians, and their misery should serve to illustrate the teachings of the church.

In the year 1215, when the Roman Catholic Church adopted the false doctrine of transubstantiation (that is, that the sacraments of the Lord's Supper become the physical substance of the body and blood of Jesus), thousands of Jews were murdered as a result. It was rumored that they covertly stole the sacraments and stuck needles into them to kill the Christ (*Anguish of the Jews,* Flannery).

Even those Jews who had converted to Christianity, under pressure and threat of persecution, were treated as second-class citizens. In Spain, they were marched into cathedrals where they were taunted in sermons, before being publicly flogged. It was unthinkable, of course, that Jews should hold any high office or possess riches. In 1492, all those Jews who had survived The Inquisition were forced to leave Spanish territory, without notice or property.

In other lands, their only refuges were in tiny, cramped and overcrowded ghettos, where at any moment they could be expelled or massacred by an impulsive governor. In Poland and Russia, Jews often lived in lowly country villages. Nevertheless, they were frequently harassed in the pogroms (with the consent of the Tsar and the Russian Orthodox Church) when hundreds, sometimes thousands of Jews were beaten to death.

Everywhere the charges were the same: They're different. They're unreliable. Disloyal. And above all: They are eternally damned for murdering the Christ!

Murderers of Christ—A False Charge

The last accusation is the most serious because it has a theological root. But is it true? Did the Jews murder Jesus? In the history of theology, Jews are often referred to as the ones who crucified Jesus and so rejected Him. Consciously or otherwise, a theologically based hatred toward Jews has taken root.

Besides this anti-Semitic view, many people accepted replacement theology, which spiritualizes the promises in the Old Testament. It takes them over and shuts out the Jews, unless, of course, they become Christians like everyone else. But is this justifiable, is it biblical, is it kind? The answer is definitely No!

First: Jesus was executed when the Jewish Council handed Him over to the Roman authorities, who on shaky evidence, sentenced Him to death. The execution itself was then carried out by Roman soldiers. Jesus had thousands of followers, and probably most of the people were for Him, but because of fear (a fairly common ailment!) they did not dare protest.

According to history then, both Romans and Jews were involved. So if we are to be consistent, all Romans and Italians ought to be persecuted because they were the ones who drove in the nails. As previously mentioned, only a few Jews were implicated. Even the Jewish Council was divided. We know that at least Nicodemus and Joseph of Arimathea were against Jesus' execution.

Second: From a theological point of view, Jesus was to be the Lamb who *would* be sacrificed for the sins of all mankind. Who, then, killed Him? Everyone, in every nation, because everyone has sinned! It was sin, committed by every sinner, that caused the crucifixion. Are we then to persecute everyone who has sin in their life? If this is so, then begin with yourself!

Jesus repeatedly told His disciples that He had to go to Jerusalem to suffer and die there. Much earlier, John the Baptist had prophesied over Him saying, *Look, the lamb of God, who takes away the sin of the world* (John 1:29). When Peter tried to defend Jesus' life with a sword in Gethsemane, Jesus declared:

> Do you think I cannot call on my Father, and he will at once put at my disposal more than twelve legions of angels? But how then would the Scriptures be fulfilled that say it must happen in this way? (Matt 26:53-54).

Jesus also said:

> The reason my Father loves me is that I lay down my life only to take it up again. *No one takes it from me, but I lay it down of my own accord.* I have authority to lay it down and authority to take it up again. This command I received from my Father (John 10:17-18).

Constantly, Jesus pointed to the necessity of His death. It was a prophesied and predetermined sacrifice for the sins of all mankind. He emphasized that He laid down His life voluntarily; no one took it from Him. Therefore, it is a hideous distortion of the truth to point out *one* nation alone and hold it solely responsible for Jesus' death.

God was the one who wanted Jesus to die. For it was only through Jesus' death as our substitute, offered for our sin and guilt, that all the sins of the world could be atoned for before Him. Jesus' sacrifice was entirely voluntary. He did it out of His love for mankind. No one took His life; He gave it.

Third: Is there any room, then, for vengeance and hate? Not at all! According to the Bible, *Love...keeps no record of wrongs* (1 Cor 13:5). No believer can ever claim that any form of personal revenge, reprisal or religious persecution is biblical.

Fourth: The Bible does not say that the Church has taken over the promises and that they no longer apply to the Jews. Neither does it say that the Jews are eternally damned, following the destruction of the second temple. This is complete nonsense and a grave misuse of the Scriptures. On the contrary, the Bible repeatedly affirms God's everlasting love for the Jewish people.

> When you pass through the waters, I will be with you; and when you pass through the rivers, they will not sweep over you. When you walk through the fire, you will not be burned; the flames will not set you ablaze. Since you are precious and honored in my sight, and because I love you, I will give men in exchange for you, and people in exchange for your life. Do not be afraid for I am with you (Isa 43:2, 4-5).

> I ask then, Did God reject his people? By no means! I am an Israelite myself, a descendant of Abraham, from the tribe of Benjamin. God did not reject his people, whom he foreknew (Rom 11:1-2).

Verse 28 adds, *they are loved on account of the patriarchs*.

God Has Not Forgotten His People

The idea that the Church has replaced Israel is incorrect. Such teaching has created a tremendous amount of anti-Semitism, and must therefore be

challenged to its core. The Jewish people are, and
will continue to be, God's chosen people. God has
never changed His mind.

Furthermore, the covenant God made with them
is everlasting.

> This is what the Lord says, he who appoints the sun
> to shine by day, who decrees the moon and stars to
> shine by night.... Only if these decrees vanish from
> my sight, declares the Lord, will the descendants of
> Israel ever cease to be a nation before me (Jer 31:35-36).

How then can Christians have the audacity to say
that God is no longer interested in the Jewish people?

We cannot deal with replacement theology in every
detail here. Others have already done it. It is enough
to say that the Church is not called Israel in the
New Testament. Seventy-seven times the names
Israel and Israelite are used in the New Testament.
On only two of these occasions is there any link
with the Church, and these two references have
commonly been misunderstood and misused.

The Church is the Church and the Jewish people,
Israel, are the Jewish people. However, Paul makes
it exceedingly plain that the believers of Gentile
birth have been blessed by being *grafted in...and
now share in the nourishing sap from the olive root*
(Rom 11:17). This is another attitude entirely! You
are a partner by grace, in someone else's blessing.
What joy! What gratitude!

The biblical promises to Israel were never given
to you. But by grace, you can claim them for yourself
too. However, this does not mean you have the right
to say they no longer belong to Israel. They do,
forever.

We have frequently spiritualized these promises,
but this is a method of preaching, introduced by the

church fathers, to avoid reading what is written. It was a method they used to evade coming into conflict with their own anti-Semitic theology. The promises mean exactly what they say.

A Debt of Gratitude to the Jews

Had it not been for the Jewish people, the world would never have heard the Gospel! Jesus was a Jew. All His disciples were Jews! The New Testament was written by Jews!

Do you know what that means? It means you owe a great debt of gratitude for what you have received, first to God and then to His chosen people.

If some of them do not believe in Him, rejoice that you do. Never criticize or boast against them! Jews are due the same respect as any other group. After all, there are many Gentiles who are not only unbelievers, but direct enemies of the Gospel. Should they be persecuted as well?

This thinking has become so distorted and deranged and caused such extreme suffering for so many people, that it is now time the Church confessed her sins and those of her forefathers. The Church must refuse all anti-Semitism in whatever form it appears. It must remove all unbiblical thinking, theology and human doctrine that have been traditionally handed down through the generations.

4

The Regathering

*Then the Lord your God will restore your fortunes
and have compassion on you and gather you
again from all the nations where he scattered
you. Even if you have been banished to the most
distant land under the heavens, from there the
Lord your God will gather you and bring you
back* (Deut 30:3-4).

Always a Way Back

God's covenants and promises to His people are
everlasting. This means that every time the prophets
pointed the finger at Israel's acts of backsliding and
pronounced judgments on her ungodliness and sin,
they also pointed out the way back to God. God
loves His people with an everlasting love.

Jeremiah 31:3 says, *I have loved you with an
everlasting love; I have drawn you with loving-kindness.* God never says to His chosen people, Israel,
That's it! I'm finished with you! On the contrary,
even if they become scattered to the farthest part
of the heavens, He promises to regather them!

After seventy years of captivity in Babylon, the
people returned home. The prophet Daniel realized
they would return, and even predicted the timing
of the return; for he discovered what Jeremiah,
another prophet, had written. *This is what the Lord
says, When seventy years are completed for Babylon,*

*I will come to you and fulfill my gracious promise
to bring you back to this place* (Jer 29:10).

As previously mentioned, although this promise
was fulfilled to the people, not all of them chose
to return. Some of them settled in commercial
areas and strategic cities. Later, when the advance
of the Roman Empire shook Israel (the province
of Judea), the Jews were still dispersed throughout
its vast reaches. That is why James says in Acts
15:21, *For Moses has been preached in every city
from earliest times and is read in the synagogues
on every Sabbath.*

During the Babylonian captivity, synagogues arose
and came into their own and spread throughout the
Gentile world. In the synagogues, the Jews of the
diaspora could congregate, pray and read from the
Torah. It was the Jews of the diaspora, present in
Jerusalem on the Day of Pentecost who said of
themselves:

> Parthians, Medes and Elamites; residents of Mesopo-
> tamia, Judea and Cappadocia, Pontus and Asia,
> Phrygia and Pamphylia, Egypt and the parts of Libya
> near Cyrene; visitors from Rome (both Jews and
> converts to Judaism); Cretans and Arabs we hear them
> declaring the wonders of God in our own tongues!
> (Acts 2:9-11).

Next Year in Jerusalem

They came, as the Scripture commanded, to celebrate
Shavuot, or Pentecost, from Asia, Africa and Europe.
They came from wherever they had been scattered
throughout the world, to celebrate the feasts in
Jerusalem and to visit the temple.

However, in AD 70 when Titus sacked the city
and burned the temple to the ground, the Jewish

people were again uprooted and scattered to the winds. Then, in AD 135, after Bar Kochba's attempted uprising failed, things looked utterly impossible. Jews were barred from Jerusalem (which was renamed) and even its proximity. Thus, the great dispersion began.

For hundreds of years, the Jewish people were spread throughout the earth. Yet wherever they settled, certain factors united them; partly, of course, their Jewishness, partly the synagogue and the law, and partly their longing to return to Israel.

They were incessantly subjected to injustice, harassed and relentlessly pursued. Wherever they settled, they were totally at the mercy of other powers. In some countries they were not sure from day to day whether they would be able to stay, or if they had to quickly pack and flee. In other countries, many were assimilated, and so partially or wholly disappeared as an ethnic-group.

Some broke with their Jewish background, simply to survive, finding that baptism in the church was often a ticket into the realm of European culture, where they hoped they would be recognized and accepted. They thought they would be able take part in cultural life, practice a trade and live as normal people.

However, at the same time, they knew they were not in their homeland. Every year at Passover (Easter) they would say to each other, Next year in Jerusalem. The hope of returning to the land that God had given them never died.

Persecution frequently arose in the countries where they settled, whether it was in Spain, Italy, England, Germany, Poland or Russia. Racial enmity, prejudice and fear created a breeding ground for militant anti-Semitism. Replacement theology in the Catholic and Orthodox churches, which was later passed on to Protestant denominations, added to this hatred of the Jews. Thus, despite the teaching of the Word of God, the official church decried and persecuted the Jewish people.

However, in spite of the theology of the Catholic church fathers, which spelled suffering and misery for many thousands of Jews, God still had His hand on them. True, the Scriptures spoke of dispersion, but they also spoke of return and restoration!

> In that day the Lord will reach out his hand a second time to reclaim the remnant that is left of his people from Assyria, from Lower Egypt, from Upper Egypt, from Cush, from Elam, from Babylonia, from Hamath and from the islands of the sea. He will raise a banner for the nations and gather the exiles of Israel; he will assemble the scattered people of Judah from the four quarters of the earth (Isa 11:11-12).

God did not plan to regather His people on only one occasion and from one land (Babylon). He would bring His people back *a second time...from the four corners of the earth*. This means that wherever Jews are living, the Spirit of God is preparing and drawing them to return to their land.

> This is what the Sovereign Lord says: I will gather you from the nations and bring you back from the countries where you have been scattered, and I will give you back the land of Israel again (Ezek 11:17).

> For *I will* take you out of the nations; I will gather you from *all* the countries and bring you back into *your own* land (Ezek 36:24).

What is God saying here? He is saying that wherever the Jews have gone and wherever they have settled,

He will bring them back! Why? Because His covenant with His people is forever!

The distinguishing feature of the Jewish people is that they have the stamp of God's eternal purposes upon them. Their position can be likened to a triangle in which the first point is the people, the second is the land and the apex is God Himself. Without the land, God cannot accomplish His purpose to bless mankind. To fulfill His will, God must have both the land and the Jewish people.

This is not just a matter of a nation's individual rights. It is a question of a people with an everlasting calling from God. Without the land, the calling cannot be realized, and without God, the people cannot fulfill their true role. This is why, when dealing with His people, God begins with the land.

Today The Unbelievable is Happening

We read in Isaiah 43:4-5, that the Lord will regather His people *since you are precious and honored in my sight and because I love you.... Do not be afraid, for I am with you; I will bring your children from the east and gather you from the west.*

But, in what way is He with them? He is with them in their regathering from every nation. According to this scripture they will be coming from the east, the west, the north and the south.

> I will say to the north, Give them up! and to the south, Do not hold them back. Bring my sons from afar and my daughters from the ends of the earth (v. 6).

This is exactly what is happening today! A hundred years ago, people would have laughed and shaken their heads in disbelief if someone had said that

Israel would be an independent land, and that Jews from all over the world would emigrate there in the *aliyah* (the return to the homeland of Israel). No one would have believed that thousands of Russians and Ethiopians would fly home. But today this is a reality.

The Jews are still very much the beloved people of God and exceedingly precious to Him. They are the apple of His eye (Deut 32:10).

Having lived for nearly 2,000 years scattered among the heathen nations, the Jews are now on their way home. On their way, because they have not all arrived yet. Ezekiel did not prophesy that only a few, or a remnant, would return. He prophesied to the land itself:

> But you, O mountains of Israel, will produce branches and fruit for my people Israel, for they will soon come home. I am concerned for you and will look on you with favor; you will be plowed and sown, and I will multiply the number of people upon you, even the whole house of Israel. The towns will be inhabited and the ruins rebuilt (Ezek 36:8-10).

What is Ezekiel saying here? He is saying they will reassemble! How will it happen? Well, it seemed inconceivable in the nineteenth century, that a land by the name of Israel would ever arise. Yet today that land is a reality. What was unbelievable then, is a fact of life now. The regathering has only just begun!

The background to the return is tragic. There has never been permanent security for the Jewish people. In Russia, where the tsars and the Orthodox church had kept a militant, anti-Semitic tradition alive, persecution and pogroms flared up at regular intervals. Tens of thousands of Jews were slaughtered and still more were banished from their homes and villages during incessant, enforced displacements.

Among these Russian Jews, and among the Polish Jews, hated by the Catholics, the thought of Zion, their homeland, began to grow even stronger. However, assimilated Jews were not interested. Orthodox Jews simply prayed and waited for the Messiah to do it for them.

But a new generation arose. It was a generation of hardy pioneers, of many atheists and socialists, but all had one burning desire—a longing to return to their ancient homeland.

Modern Zionism

Such were the roots of modern Zionism. The name we link most closely with it is that of Theodore Herzl, an Austrian journalist living in Vienna. Due to Vienna's strongly anti-Semitic atmosphere, Herzl had conformed to the society around him. (Somewhat later, Hitler experienced this same anti-Semitic atmosphere while wandering the streets as a penniless artist.)

Herzl was sent to Paris by his newspaper, *Neue Freie Presse,* to cover the scandalous court case against Alfred Dreyfus, a captain in the French army, and a Jew. Dreyfus was charged with high treason and of having used his position on the general staff to divulge secrets to the Germans. Herzl was present at Dreyfus' degradation, and heard as the mob outside began howling Death to Dreyfus! Death to the Jews!

He was shaken to the core. Writing later, he said that the whole of his Jewish heritage awoke within him. After pacing the streets of Paris for several more days, Theodore Herzl returned home, an entirely different man. A few months later he completed his book, *Der Judenstaat* (The Jewish State), which was to become the manifesto of modern Zionism.

Der Judenstaat was the compilation of the dreams of many a Jew, and a trumpet call to Zionism. On August 29, 1897, delegations from sixteen countries met in Basel, Germany, for the first Zionist congress. Afterward, Herzl wrote in his diary: I created the Jewish State in Basel. If I said so out loud today, I'd be laughed at everywhere. Maybe in five years, but in any case fifty, everyone will know it.

The Balfour Declaration

Zionism increased rapidly. Jews from many different backgrounds joined, united by the common need for a homeland of their own—Eretz Israel.

At that time, the land of Israel was part of the Ottoman Empire, ruled by the Turks. However, in 1917, the First World War broke out and the British fought the Turks in the Middle East. Two significant events took place: the British took Jerusalem, under General Allenby, and the Turks lost Palestine.

Shortly afterwards, Palestine was established by British mandate. Through its colonial minister, Arthur James Balfour, the British government consented to the establishment of a national home in Palestine for the Jewish people, and issued what is now known as the Balfour Declaration.

This document provided legal status to the Jews' endeavors to return to their ancient homeland. As described in the Balfour Declaration, Palestine was an extensive mandate, or area, including both Israel and Jordan as they are today. In other words, the whole of this area was intended to become a national home for the Jews.

Of course, Arab nationalism could not tolerate this arrangement, and put pressure on the British government to break its promise. The Palestinian mandate was thus divided so that everything east of the River Jordan, over 70 per cent of the whole area, became Trans Jordan, an Arab country (later, Jordan). Little more than 20 per cent remained.

Fears that this small part might fall to the Jews caused increased Arab resistance to immigration, in the form of persecution and pogroms. Arab immigration was simultaneously stepped up and Jewish immigration was drastically limited by the British. After a time, the so-called White Papers were issued. Their purpose was to placate the Arabs by limiting Jewish immigration.

Nazism

During the 1930's, dark clouds began to gather over Europe. God's movement, to regather His people into their land, was gaining momentum, but so too, was anti-Semitism. Persecution of Jews was becoming more spiteful.

In Germany, Hitler came to power in 1933 and two years later he issued the Nuremburg decrees, which denied German Jews any legal or citizen's rights. Their plight grew increasingly desperate. They were harassed, arrested, plundered and murdered.

In 1938, an international conference was convened in Evian, France, where the Jewish situation was discussed. No country, however, was prepared to open its doors for a German Jew. Despite their knowledge of the situation, *no land* was willing to make the slightest move to change it.

Instead, they all turned their backs, looked away and allowed the Jews to head toward a tragic fate. Hitler had been given the world's silent consent. No one wanted anything to do with the Jews. He was now free to vent his murderous hatred on them, unrestrained. Thus, the true face of Nazism became increasingly seen, as the Second World War continued.

In 1942, at the Wannsee meeting in Berlin, a decision was made concerning The Final Solution to the Jewish Question. In plain language, this meant full permission to proceed with the total annihilation of all European Jews.

As time went on, the holocaust was given increasing priority, even over the battles themselves. The longer the war progressed, and long after their fortunes turned, the Nazis worked feverishly, herding Jews together, dispatching them, forcing them into concentration camps such as Auschwitz, Sobibor and Dachau, and murdering them. This mass murder of some six million Jews is indisputably the worst outrage in world history.

There are no words to describe the suffering it inflicted. It is impossible to depict the wretchedness and misery in its wake. That it was perpetrated at all, is heinous. That it was committed by a nation that was considered the cultural elite of Europe, is incomprehensible; and that it was done by Christians, is a shame beyond words.

The renowned Nazi hunter, Simon Wiesenthal, has described how he was rescued from the bullets of a firing squad. While he stood there in a line awaiting execution, and Jews died beside him, the soldiers suddenly stopped shooting. They had heard church bells, and took a break from the killing while they went to vespers.

How can a Jew who has gone through these things ever believe in a Christian again? Especially since the Christian church, Christian theologians and Christian countries have led the field in anti-Semitism.

Anti-Semitism After 1945

At last the war came to an end. The concentration camps were opened, and survivors stumbled out bearing testimonies of things more cruel than people were prepared to believe, or could even bear to hear. In any case, the atrocities were well documented so that coming generations would not forget.

Sadly, this has not hindered a few anti-Semitic, so-called historians from trying to deny the holocaust and rewrite history. As recently as the spring of 1992, one such revisionist named Robert Faurisson was invited to Sweden by the Muslim, Ahmed Rami of Radio Islam, in an attempt to spread his venomous lies.

When the world at large became aware of the outrages of the holocaust, there was a basis for the creation of a Jewish state in Palestine. The survivors wanted to go to their ancient homeland. The Jews who had immigrated earlier, and lived in the Palestinian Mandate during the Second World War, worked intensely. They wanted to get their Jewish brothers home, and get the world to acknowledge the need for a Jewish national home, as promised by the Balfour Declaration.

At this point, several remarkable things happened. Many of the Jews who had been freed from the concentration camps, especially in Poland, met with intense resistance. In anti-Semitic Poland, several pogroms took place *after the war.* Despite all that had happened during the war, hatred toward Jews was still to be found among the Poles. Many Jews were murdered as a result.

Even Britain, which had defeated Germany, continued to yield to pressure from the Arabs and to Arab anti-Semitism.

The Double-dealing and Downfall of Britain

The British had appointed a religious leader for the Muslims in Palestine, the Great Mufti, Haj Amin el-Husseini. He was a rabid Jew hater and stirred up aggression against them. During the war, he took a clear stand in favor of Nazism, and for several years, lived in Berlin. He became a friend of Hitler, Himmler and Eichmann, visited concentration camps and counted on the help of the Germans to kill all the Jews in Palestine.

As we know, Germany lost the war, but Britain never clearly sided with the Jews. During the war, the concentration camps could easily have been bombed, but they never were. The White Papers, that were drawn up to hinder the illegal immigration of Jews to Palestine, could have been repealed, but they were not. Britain could have encouraged the formation of the State of Israel, but it never did.

Britain sided with the Arabs instead. It did everything to impede surviving Jews from reassembling in their land at the end of the war. Ships carrying survivors were forced to heave to (as in the case of the Exodus), and those on board were stopped from disembarking in Palestine. Illegal immigrants were caught and penalized. Those who had just been freed from concentration camps in Germany, were concentrated in camps on Cyprus.

Britain had made a fatal mistake in this. Genesis 12:3 says, *I will bless those who bless you, and whoever curses you I will curse; and all peoples on earth will be blessed through you.* Through its actions, Britain, the victor of the war, brought a curse on itself. Within a few years, Britain would lose its status as conqueror, its glory, its empire and its economy; appearing instead as a land full of difficulties and problems.

In its Middle East policy, Britain had done its utmost to foil the development of a Jewish state. Not even this aim was attained. On November 29, 1947, the newly formed United Nations voted in its general assembly that the Palestinian Mandate, which had been given up by Britain, was to be divided into two parts: A Jewish state and an Arab State. The votes were 33 for, 13 against and 10 abstentions. The Jews rejoiced, the Arabs were furious; Britain voted against.

At Last, a Land of their Own!

On May 14, 1948, Prime Minister Ben Gurion officially proclaimed a Jewish state under the name Israel. After nearly 2,000 years the Jews were now home again, just as God had promised!

> I will choose one of you from every town and two from every clan and bring you to Zion (Jer 3:14).

When the survivors of the holocaust arrived in their infant Israel, this was exactly what they found: one or two survivors from each town and village, with roots in each tribe. In many towns, whole Jewish populations had been eradicated. Where there had formerly been life and bustling Jewish activity, no one was left. The few Jews who had outlived the holocaust knew that the only real security that could be offered them was a land of their own.

If they had possessed Israel immediately after the First World War, they would have had a land of their own, a refuge place from Nazi anti-Semitism. But there was no Israel then, and no country was willing to offer them a helping hand. Commenting on the question of opening up the country to take in Jews, the Prime Minister of Canada answered, One Jew to Canada, is one too many.

Islam to the Attack

However, a state of their own was at last a reality, despite resistance. But as soon as independence was proclaimed, Israel was plunged into war. During the Second World War, Jewish settlers in the Palestinian Mandate had fought with the British army. Now, her former soldiers and prisoners from concentration camps were instantly thrown into battle.

The surrounding Arab states numbered some forty million inhabitants, and not one of them wanted a non-Muslim country as a neighbor. Under shouts of Death to the Jews and Throw them into the sea, the infant state was immediately attacked. Age-old anti-Semitism had been given a new face—Muslim anti-Semitism and anti-Zionism. It was a miracle that the infant state of Israel survived.

Politicians throughout the world had declared Israel dead, giving it no chance. Theologians in many circles proclaimed that modern Israel had nothing to do with ancient Israel. Replacement theology trained its sights on the tiny Jewish state. The Catholic church refused to recognize the young state, and to this day the Vatican has never acknowledged Israel, because it sees itself as the new Israel and lays claim to its territory.

However, God had other thoughts. He acknowledged Israel. He gathered the people, and He miraculously gave them their land.

> Before she goes into labor, she gives birth; before the pains come upon her, she delivers a son. Who has ever heard of such a thing? Who has ever seen such things? Can a country be born in a day or a nation be brought forth in a moment? Yet no sooner is Zion in labor than she gives birth to her children (Isa 66:7-8).

The land sprang to life on a single day! Many predicted that it would be overrun by the Arabs within weeks. How could it possibly cope against such overwhelming odds? But it did. It survived and the Arabs were defeated. The Jews had returned to their land, never to leave it again.

> I will plant Israel in their own land, *never again* to be uprooted from the land I have given them, says the Lord your God (Amos 9:15).

When they returned, it was forever, never to be uprooted again. This was the reason the Arabs, though vastly superior in numbers, did not succeed in throwing the Jews into the sea. It is also the reason they will never succeed. They are fighting God Himself, and he who fights God will always lose!

Through the Fire

With the proclamation of the Jewish state, wave after wave of immigration followed, and war followed war. After the War of Independence came the Suez

Crisis, then the Six Day War, the Yom Kippur War, the Lebanon War and, most recently, the Gulf War. Not one of Israel's neighbors has made peace, only cessation of hostilities, followed by new acts of aggression. In spite of this, Jews have returned to their homeland from all over the world.

> But now, this is what the Lord says he who created you, O Jacob, he who formed you, O Israel: Fear not, for I have redeemed you; I have called you by name; you are mine. When you pass through the waters, I will be with you; and when you pass through the rivers, they will not sweep over you. When you walk through the fire, you will not be burned; the flames will not set you ablaze. For I am the Lord, your God, the Holy One of Israel, your Savior; I give Egypt for your ransom, Cush and Sheba in your stead. Since you are precious and honored in my sight, and because I love you, I will give men in exchange for you, and people in exchange for your life. Do not be afraid, for I am with you; I will bring your children from the east and gather you from the west. I will say to the north, 'Give them up!' and to the south, 'Do not hold them back.' Bring my sons from afar and my daughters from the ends of the earth everyone who is called by my name, whom I created for my glory, whom I formed and made (Isa 43:1-7).

The immigrants came from the east: from Iran and Iraq. Unique operations were carried out, rescuing tens of thousands of Jews from hostile Arab states. They also came from the west: from the USA, Britain, France and Germany. Immigrants came from the south: from South Africa, Yemen and Ethiopia. They also came from the north, though not so many: from the Soviet Union.

Millions of Jews were to be found within the borders of the Soviet Union, but they were unable to leave. Therefore, it is significant to see what the Lord says in Isaiah 43:6, *I will say to the north, Give them up!*

God put it in the hearts of many to pray that the Russian Jews would come out. He sent delegation after delegation into the Soviet Union to pray and ask the authorities to open its borders. However, atheistic communism put up fierce resistance to the fulfilling of God's prophetic promises.

This is why the Scriptures take on a commanding tone, declaring *Give them up!* Nothing can withstand the command of God. Glasnost and Perestroika made their appearance. In Germany, the Berlin Wall fell and the whole communistic system collapsed. Doors to the Soviet Union were thrown wide open for two reasons: The Gospel was to go in and the Jews were to come out!

> The days are coming, declares the Lord, when men will no longer say, 'As surely as the Lord lives, who brought the Israelites up out of Egypt,' but they will say, 'As surely as the Lord lives, *who brought the Israelites up out of the land of the north* and out of all the countries where he had banished them.' For I will restore them to the land I gave their forefathers (Jer 16:14-15).

Out of the North

Here, the Lord is referring to a new exodus, far greater than the escape from Egypt. The exodus from Egypt was certainly the most outstanding miracle of the Old Testament. It enjoys a distinct and prominent place among all the festivals held by the Jews, who celebrate it every Passover (Easter). But now the Lord says that something else is going to happen that will totally eclipse that mighty miracle.

A new exodus will take place from another direction—the north. North of Israel is different from north of Rome, north of New York or north of Stockholm. North of Israel is north of Jerusalem, and directly north of Jerusalem lies Moscow. The north and the far north are called Russia today.

Since the fall of the Soviet Union, thousands of Russian Jews have returned to Israel. Tremendous and inconceivable as it is, this is still not what Jeremiah 16:14-15 is talking about. There, the Lord speaks about a greater and more dramatic exodus than that from Egypt. It has not yet taken place, but it will, with all certainty.

The situation in Russia and other former Soviet republics will prove to be such that a dramatic exodus of Jews will take place. The political situation is unstable and subject to change. The financial state of affairs is near disaster. In circumstances such as these, people look for a scapegoat and the Jews have often been picked on before.

In Russia there is a tradition of anti-Semitism because of the Russian Orthodox Church. Deep in the minds of the people lies a prejudice toward Jews. Communistic anti-Semitism, which was extremely vocal during Stalin's time, has roots reaching far back into the time of the tsars. New nationalistic religious groups, such as Pamjat, are confirmed Jew haters.

Therefore, it is immensely important to pray for a genuine revival in Russia. Russia needs a revival which will give rise to true evangelical, biblical faith; rather than vain religious imaginations, superstitions or unenlightened and preconceived ideas.

In Russia, as in every other country, it is essential to warn against the resurgence of anti-Semitism. On several occasions I have had the privilege of preaching to thousands of Russians, and I have issued a stern warning against anti-Semitism. I have encouraged young churches to bless Israel instead, and to help Jews return home to their land.

Besides simply knowing about the coming exodus, it is also important to prepare for it practically, so the people can leave Russia quickly, when the time arrives.

When people doubt the authenticity of the Bible and its relevance for present realities, it is often due to their over concentration on the political situations of the moment. However, every day, situations change rapidly. Who foresaw the collapse of the Soviet Union, the fall of the Berlin Wall or the reunification of Germany, a few years ago? But these are facts today.

> Praise be to the name of God for ever and ever; wisdom and power are his. He changes times and seasons; he sets up kings and deposes them. He gives wisdom to the wise and knowledge to the discerning (Dan 2:20-21).

Spiritual Blindness

Another reason for doubt in the lives of believers, is that many have embraced a gnosticly inspired philosophy which teaches them to believe that God does not intervene in history. However, this is not what the Bible teaches. The God of Israel, the God of Abraham, Isaac and Jacob, is the God of history. He breaks into history and He writes history. He changes history and, through His prophets, He foretells history.

Those Christian denominations that deny both the authenticity of the Bible and the basic tenets of the faith, are those that fight two things today: revival among Christians, and Israel.

Furthermore, those politicians who do not accept biblical revelation are the most anti-Semitic and anti-Zionistic. This is because, in denying the truth, they have thrown away the key to understanding history, its setting, its sequence and its end. Consequently, they stand perplexed and nonplused in the face of Middle East problems.

This is also why they are frequently frustrated with Israel, prejudiced in their views toward it and have often taken the wrong side. How many politicians are there who have not bowed to Arab pressure, oil boycotts, trade embargoes and even terrorism, while believing they were serving the purpose of peace? In reality, they were creating more trouble by falling into a situation where they were resisting God and His blessings and plans.

The most recent example of this is the USA. Once a staunch friend of Israel, it has increasingly distanced itself, through pressure from the Arabs and other short-sighted interests. The real turning point came when President Bush came to power. If the USA continues on this new course, pressurizing Israel to give up the land it annexed after the Six Day War, the world will witness the decline and fall of the United States, just as it has witnessed the fall of every other world power that has either forsaken or gone against Israel.

The salvation of Israel does not lie in the blessing of the USA, it lies in the Lord. On the other hand, the salvation of the USA lies in blessing Israel.

5

Muslim Anti-Semitism

Throughout history, the Jewish people have suffered unparalleled hatred and persecution. To those without spiritual understanding, this may seem quite mystifying. How can a single nation be blamed for so many different things?

Some accuse them of capitalism, others accuse them of communism. Some complain that they infiltrate nations, others complain that they keep themselves apart. In each situation, the charges appear to be adapted to the issues of the day, but always with the same result: the Jews become the scapegoat.

After the Second World War, when the State of Israel was born, a decisive change took place. The Nazis were defeated and the Jews' ancient hope of being able to return to their homeland was now a reality. After nearly 2,000 years of banishment and dispersion, the people began to turn homeward again. In many ways, the future seemed bright. Unfortunately, it was not to prove so simple.

As Jewish immigration increased, so did Arab opposition. The surrounding Arab nations, also young states, were impelled by the pan-Arab idea; that is, that the entire Middle East should become one, large Arab nation. It was absolutely unthinkable to have a Jewish State right in the middle of it.

So in 1947, every Arab nation voted against the United Nations' plan to divide the former British mandate. Somewhat reluctantly, the Jews accepted the UN compromise. This created both a Jewish and an Arab state within the former British mandate, although the entire geographical area had been promised to the Jews from the beginning by the Balfour Declaration.

Arab rejection of the proposition, however, was outright. Therefore, in 1948 when Israel was proclaimed an independent nation, an instant offensive was launched to annihilate the newborn state. Since then, peace has never been declared; only cessation of hostilities.

The only exception is Egypt, which made a separate peace pact with Israel after the Yom Kippur war (1973). Because of this act, however, Egypt was immediately and totally ostracized by the Arab community.

From the beginning, there have been many border infringements, terrorist attacks and acts of sabotage against Israel. There are endless oil boycotts and trade embargoes, and nations which trade with Israel have come under great pressure. Slander, negative propaganda, international isolation and incessant preparation for new wars, are only a few of the weapons used against her—not to mention the actual wars that have been waged since her independence.

Onlookers must ask themselves: Why all this aversion, and why this hatred of Israel? The answer is that anti-Semitism, with its age-old prejudices and hatred, previously directed at the Jewish diaspora, has now shifted its attention to the state of Israel itself.

Anti-Semitism—A Demonic Power!

Today, anti-Semitism masquerades under a new name, Anti-Zionism. Nowadays you can hear people say, I'm not anti-Semitic, I'm only anti-Zionistic! But what does that mean? It means, Well, all right, let the Jews exist if they must, as long as they don't hold on to their identity, their history or their homeland.

If Israel lays claim to a part, or worse, to the whole of her ancient homeland, she is depicted in the most spiteful terms. Jews are portrayed as neo-Nazis, as fifth-columnists, etc. But why? What lies behind it all? Whose purposes are being served?

First, it is important to clarify that behind anti-Semitism lies a powerful evil spirit, a demon prince, a satanic principality. It shifts about from nation to nation and from culture to culture. It adopts many faces, but retains one goal: the all-out obstruction of the Jews to prevent them from entering into their divine role and calling.

For this calling to be fulfilled, the people must exist, the land must exist, and God must exist! All are necessary, for it is within the land that the people are to complete their commission, which is, to serve God. Take away the people, the land, or faith in God, and the calling will be lost and along with it, the blessing to the rest of mankind. Therefore, the enemy concentrates his attacks on these three areas.

This demon power is described in Daniel 10:12-11:1:

Then he continued, Do not be afraid, Daniel. Since the first day that you set your mind to gain understanding and to humble yourself before your God, your words were heard, and I have come in response to them. But the prince of the Persian kingdom resisted me twenty-one days. Then Michael, one of the chief princes, came to help me, because I was detained there with the king of Persia. Now I have come to explain to you what will happen to your people in the future, for the vision concerns a time yet to come. While he was saying this to me, I bowed with my face toward the ground and was speechless. Then one who looked like a man touched my lips, and I opened my mouth and began to speak. I said to the one standing before me, I am overcome with anguish because of the vision, my lord, and I am helpless. How can I, your servant, talk with you, my lord? My strength is gone and I can hardly breathe. Again the one who looked like a man touched me and gave me strength. Do not be afraid, O man highly esteemed, he said. Peace! Be strong now; be strong. When he spoke to me, I was strengthened and said, Speak, my lord, since you have given me strength. So he said, Do you know why I have come to you? Soon I will return to fight against the prince of Persia, and when I go, the prince of Greece will come; but first I will tell you what is written in the Book of Truth. (No one supports me against them except Michael, your prince. And in the first year of Darius the Mede, I took my stand to support and protect him.)

The Middle East—A Spiritual Problem

According to the book of Daniel, spirit powers, or principalities, withstood the Angel Gabriel as he winged God's answer to Daniel, who was in prayer. He was praying that the people would be given their liberty to return home to their land. The same spirit powers are active today, hindering the Jewish people from returning home; for it is there in Israel that they will fulfill their calling.

The Jews and Israel may be supported on humanitarian grounds, but such sympathy is superficial. It does not go deep enough. The people cannot be considered separately from God, nor can they be dealt with apart from the land.

When politicians show goodwill toward Israel, yet simultaneously demand that they give up the so-called West Bank (that is, Judea and Samaria) and East Jerusalem, it simply reveals that they have no understanding of the problem.

The Jews are the people of the Book, the people of the Bible. Israel is the land of the Bible, *the promised land*. Without an understanding of these points of reference, the problems of the Middle East are incomprehensible.

This very ignorance leads some to accuse the Israelis of being stubborn, undiplomatic and obstinate, and of being different from other nations, because they will not voluntarily give up their territory or be talked into compromise. But how can they? They would be denying their very calling! Furthermore, outside the land they have no sure security or protection.

Islam's Hatred of Israel

Israel is an island surrounded by a sea of Arab peoples. Every Arab state is hostile toward it. Its peace treaty with Egypt is fragile and there have been frequent skirmishes over the borders. But are these problems simply territorial or ethnic? No, it is not that simple. Behind Arab hostility there lies a religion, Islam.

Every year the Muslims have a month of fasting, Ramadan. In Iran, and all over the world, the last day of the fast is ended by spells and curses being uttered against the State of Israel. Muslims throughout the world are summoned, indoctrinated with incredible prejudices, and incited to an irreconcilable hatred toward Israel. Time-worn anti-Semitism has now found a new face, that of Islam.

To understand Islam, one must go back to its founder, Mohammed, who was born into the Quarish tribe in Mecca in AD 570. While still very young he was orphaned, and consequently he was brought up by his uncle. In his youth, the young Mohammed came into contact with Jews and various groups of Christians.

In the year AD 610 an angel by the name of Jibrib appeared to Mohammed, and presented to him a god called Allah. After this calling at the age of 40, Mohammed began to preach his faith in Allah, who was one of the many desert gods venerated at the time. Allah was the jackal god.

Mohammed promoted this wilderness god to the position of the one and only god. He outlawed polytheism by ordering obeisance to Allah alone, and saw himself as Allah's ultimate prophet. According to him, Allah was the same as the God of the Jews and the Christians. However, as time passed, it became increasingly clear that this was not the case.

The revelations that Mohammed wrote down during his angelic visitations are found in the Koran. Their content is substantially divergent from that of the Bible, and in many places completely contradictory.

A short summary of Islam would read: Islam is an anti-religion, a contra-religion, written against Jewry and against Christendom, and in no way reminiscent of the Judeo-Christian revelation of the Lord. The character of the God of the Bible bears no trace of similarity to the character of Allah, the god of Islam. Allah is not the same god at all.

God Gave the Revelation of Himself to Israel

When God created man, He set eternity in his heart. *He has made everything beautiful in its time. He has also set eternity in the hearts of men* (Eccl 3:11). When man sinned and fell, his concept of God became dim. He was, nevertheless, still able to appreciate God's existence in two ways: through nature and through his conscience (see Rom 1:19-20 and 2:14-15).

If a man violates his conscience, his mind becomes darkened. Romans 1:21 tells us, *For although they knew God, they neither glorified him as God nor gave thanks to him, but their thinking became futile and their foolish hearts were darkened.* The result of this darkening of the mind, the Bible says, is the setting up of idols that are venerated and worshiped in place of the One True God (see Rom 1:22-25).

Behind these idols and their worship lie demonic powers. *The sacrifices of pagans are offered to demons, not to God, and I do not want you to be participants with demons* (1 Cor 10:20) and *They sacrificed to demons, which are not God gods they had not known, gods that recently appeared, gods your fathers did not fear* (Deut 32:17).

The Bible describes how sin and disobedience caused man to provide himself with false gods in order to satisfy his inherent religious craving. He tried to placate the unknown, the uncertain and the fearsome things around him; and above all, the threat of death. At the same time, the Bible refers to man's longing for God, which is rooted deep in his conscience.

God then moved in this situation and revealed Himself to man. He imparted this revelation to the people of Israel. They were shown who He is, what he desires, and how man can come to Him. And

God chose the people of Israel because he wanted to do so!

This revelation was faithfully and meticulously written down in the Bible for all of mankind, forever. No one can approach God without this revelation. God's love is seen in His willingness and ability to reveal Himself to mankind. He gave His revelation to the children of Israel who were to steward and spread it.

In Romans 9:4 Paul says of the Jewish people, *Theirs is the adoption as sons; theirs the divine glory, the covenants, the receiving of the law, the temple worship and the promises.* In other words, it was to them that God gave His revelation of Himself.

The Koran Tells Untruths

When a person either does not know or accept the revelation God has given him, his mind becomes darkened and he begins to create his own gods. Vain thoughts arise in his mind against the knowledge of the One True God (2 Cor 10:5), and he comes under the influence of religious spirit powers, which actively seduce people to worship false gods.

A closer examination of Islam reveals that it is, in fact, an anti-religion. The Koran denies that Jesus is the Son of God, the Savior of the world and the cornerstone of the Christian faith. It denies that Jesus died on the cross, saying that He was taken up to heaven before the crucifixion, and that another body, similar to His, died on the cross instead. Therefore, according to Islam, Jesus' blood possesses no redeeming power or virtue at all.

The Koran's description of Jesus' birth also diverges wholly from that of the New Testament. Its story of Abraham is equally strange. According to the Koran, Abraham had eight sons whom he brought up in Mecca, not Hebron; the blessing of Allah was passed on from Abraham through Ishmael, not Isaac; and it was Ishmael, not Isaac, whom Abraham was about to offer as a sacrifice.

The Koran also makes other historical errors, for example: Moses was adopted by Pharaoh's wife, not his daughter; Haman was a minister of Pharaoh's government in Egypt, not in Persia; the mother of Jesus was Miriam the sister of Moses, not Mary, and so on. In other words, the Koran is full of contradictions and lies.

But how can we be certain they are lies? Because Mohammed rewrote the historical content of the Bible to adapt it to his own theories and fantasies. It hardly makes matters better that Muslims today get angry and threaten anyone who points out discrepancies in the Koran, with revenge and bloodshed.

When representatives of religion cannot manage to discuss their case reasonably, but begin to cry out and threaten with the sword, it reveals something about the content, the source and the aim of their religion.

Furthermore, the Koran contains a substantial amount of anti-Semitism. The Jews are depicted as a backslided and perverted people who curse Allah, etc. The Koran purports that Jews deliberately twist the scriptures and are rejected by God for not acknowledging the Koran as a holy book. Thus, they make themselves the enemies of Allah.

Jihad—Holy War

Mohammed himself had a strong dislike for Jews, and through him Muslim anti-Semitism came into being. When Islam was spread throughout the Saudi Arabian peninsula, a call to Jihad—holy war—was proclaimed. It meant that the Koran and the Muslim religion were to be spread with the edge of the sword and violence.

Jihad is the sixth of Islam's five pillars. The first five are:

1. The confession of the faith: There is no god but Allah, and Mohammed is his prophet.

2. Prayer (fives times a day, facing Mecca and the Kaaba stone).

3. Giving of alms.

4. Fasting, especially during the month of Ramadan, and

5. Haj, a pilgrimage to Mecca, to be made at least once in a lifetime.

According to the Koran, the world is divided into two houses: the House of Islam and the House of War. The House of War includes all the lands and nations that have not yet joined Islam. The five pillars of Islam are to be established in these lands and this will be achieved with the help of Jihad—holy war.

Where Jihad is a political impossibility, Islam is to advance by other means. But as soon as it is possible, Jihad must be the prime method, because the goal is world annexation to the House of Islam. Jihad was the key Mohammed was given for the rapid expansion of his religion. After his death, Islam spread throughout the Mediterranean and out into the world.

Massacres have been a regular feature in the extension of Islam. Any nation that did not immediately convert was pronounced *dhimmi*, infidel, and its people were made second-class citizens.

They had heavy taxes and restrictions imposed on them, and if they broke Islamic law the Koran demanded punishment by death.

The Jews were, no doubt, oppressed in lands under Muslim dominion, but they often coped better in this situation than they did later in Christian Europe and during the Crusades.

However, Islam's position was completely clear: Judaism was a corrupt religion and the Jews a rejected people. Even if they were given recognition as the people of the Book and their prophets venerated, they were, nevertheless, still enemies and would remain so as long as they refused to accept Mohammed's final revelation.

As Islam advanced geographically, new territories fell under its power. Any land that was once conquered by Islam, but later lost to other conquerors, is to be retaken by all available means. This is every Muslim's duty. Neither Palestine nor Spain, nor the Balkan Peninsula, are exceptions to this rule. The Muslim goal for any land once taken, is to make the Koran the basis for its constitution and law. Thus, the government and the Koran become one and the same, and the rise of a theocratic dictatorship is unavoidable.

Herein lies a vast difference between Islamic and Judeo-Christian thinking. The Bible and the Ten Commandments can, and ought to be, the ethical and moral basis for legislation, but it never strives for theocratic dictatorship. The opposite is true. The Bible safeguards democratic rule, democratic freedom and democratic rights, which have been made possible by its influence on society.

The Bible does not perceive society as being under the control of religious dictators but, instead, it promotes democracy, indeed, pluralism. The Church of the New Testament is an organization which is totally different to world institutions, because it is based upon faithfulness to Jesus. Its often secular surroundings rarely know or believe in Him.

Conversion, according to the Bible, is the turning of the heart to God and faith in Him. A pure and holy life is the result. Outward conversion, by political coercion and forced territorial advance, is worthless. The one is the way of God's Spirit, the other the way of human flesh.

Muslim Diplomacy

Individuality, personal responsibility and accountability, are all absent from Islam. A voluntary heart repentance is also noticeably absent and in its place is submission, which is what Islam means. Furthermore, the concepts of peace and forgiveness are nonexistent. Peace is never made, only a temporary cessation of hostilities until the outlook is more favorable, and the sword, which spreads Islam, can be taken up again.

Moreover, the concept of truth is totally alien. The Muslim has no moral duty to tell the truth or keep agreements with infidels. Therefore, pledges and peace treaties can be made and broken at will.

This is one explanation as to why Yassir Arafat can acknowledge Israel to the Western world, while denying it among his Muslim friends. He is speaking to unbelievers, infidels. The naive westerner can easily become bewildered, disappointed and deluded.

The anti-Semitic Great Mufti in Jerusalem is, in fact, Yassir Arafat's uncle, Haj Amin el-Husseini. (Yassir Arafat's full name is Abed a-Rachman Abed a-Rouf Arafat al-Qudwah el-Husseini.) Such a notorious relationship has been hushed up in the West, but the same hatred toward Jews has been passed on and is at work today through the PLO.

The current Middle East conflict does not have its roots in politics, ethnic minorities or territorial boundaries. It is a spiritual conflict and the unrelenting spirit of Islam hangs over the Arab world.

Therefore, it is humiliating for Islam to have a Jewish state as a neighbor, especially since Muslims believe Jews to be rejected by Allah.

It is important here not to allow oneself to be manipulated by liberal theological Islam researchers who frequently emphasize so-called similarities between Islam and Judeo-Christian thinking. They usually do this to tone down or completely forget the grossly disagreeable facts about Islam, since they appear so foreign and bizarre to the Western observer. But nevertheless, they are facts.

It is obvious that Islam can never, and will never, acknowledge a Jewish homeland in Palestine. This is why Arafat expresses his loathing for the Balfour Declaration. This is also why he told an Arab leader that it was good that the Berlin Wall, one of the last remnants of the Second World War, had disappeared, but that the last remnant, Israel, must also go.

Finally, Jerusalem is in Israel; and Jerusalem has been pronounced the third most holy city of Islam after Mecca and Medina, where Mohammed lived. The fact that Jerusalem is now no longer divided is a source of further animosity. After 1967, Jerusalem was proclaimed the undivided capital city of Israel.

The Demand for Jerusalem

Before 1967, while eastern Jerusalem was still in Jordanian hands, no Jew was allowed in the vicinity of the Wailing (Western) Wall. Synagogues were blown up or demolished, and Jews were banished from their ancient quarters in the Old City.

Today, however, the Israeli state guarantees Muslims access to the Temple Mount and safeguards their security while worshiping in the mosques on the site of the ancient Jewish temple. In contrast, Muslims do not allow Christians or Jews to pray there.

It is also significant that the Koran does not mention Jerusalem by name in connection with Mohammed. It says that he flew on his horse to Al Quds, from where he ascended to heaven; but it never says that Al Quds is Jerusalem. Muslim tradition added this interpretation later, probably to justify their demand for Jerusalem.

Jerusalem had never held the prominent position which they later asserted. However, the more the Jews desired to return there, the more the Muslims wanted the city. Today, the entire Muslim world once again demands Jerusalem. Unfortunately, Western politicians can hardly distinguish between the widely differing religions. They do not understand the meaning of Jerusalem to the Jews, or see through Muslim propaganda in its attempts to retake it. Instead, they offer human compromises that satisfy no one. Why? Because the basic truth is pushed to the background and the conflictive situation becomes a question of culture. In other words, politicians accept what they call cultural differences, and avoid assessing what is right and what is wrong, what is truth and what is a lie.

Communism Fell, Islam Will Fall Too

The denial of reality in the name of culture has opened the way for increased anti-Semitism. To say that all religions are alike, without informing oneself of the teaching and practices of these religions, usually has one result: the one who shouts the loudest and is most brutal is awarded the case, regardless of what is true or false.

The demands from the Muslim side are impossible. Some content themselves with saying that the Jews must leave their land, while others go as far as to say that they must leave the surface of the earth. Examples of hatred toward Jews are myriad. These range from Radio Islam's* denial of the holocaust, to Muslim suicide terrorists, with a machete in one hand and the Koran in the other, madly cutting down innocent Jews in Israel.

However, not all Arabs have this fanatical attitude. Not all Arabs want Israel annihilated. Some are happy for peaceful coexistence with Israel, living side by side with the Jews. But those who feel this way are more often than not threatened with death if they open their mouths. Extremists rule, and force the rest to silence.

And their weapons? Usually, a fanatical Muslim position! But Islam is a false religion, and as an idol, it will fall. Allah is *not* the God of the Bible. He is not the God of Abraham, Isaac and Jacob. He is a bloodthirsty, vindictive, desert god behind which an evil spirit is concealing itself.

When his power and grip are broken from off the Arab nations they will be in a similar situation to

---

* Radio Islam is a local radio broadcast in Sweden.

the former communist countries. A wall will collapse. Violence, animosity and prejudices will be broken down, and the children of Ishmael will look up to the God of Israel, the Living God. An in-depth spiritual revival is the only solution to the problem of the Middle East.

Abraham's blessing was given to all peoples, including the Arab world. When the Holy Spirit touches people's hearts, then hearts will be circumcised and Islam, with its hatred, despotism and violence, will be swept away. Then, and only then, will the thirst for blood and revenge leave, and true peace come to the Middle East.

6

Israel in the Last Days

While talking one day with Abraham, the Lord told him that his descendants would become a blessing to every family (nation) on earth. This is God's ultimate goal for Israel. The whole of mankind, and Israel herself, will reap the benefits of the blessing that God gave her through Abraham.

During the Babylonian captivity, however, it seemed as though Israel had lost her destiny. Her people had been led away as prisoners and scattered. Her land had been conquered and devastated. Jerusalem lay in ruins and the temple was demolished. But it was then, during the captivity in Babylon, that the Lord spoke to Daniel the prophet, and unfolded to him His entire prophetic blueprint for Israel and the Gentile world.

The Times of the Gentiles

Every nation mentioned in the Bible had some relationship to Israel. God has placed Israel in the center of nations to be a gauge and signpost throughout history. Each nation will be judged on how it has treated Israel, and God's plans for each nation will be developed accordingly.

The Babylonian conquest and captivity of Israel ushered in a new era—The Times of the Gentiles. From now on, Gentile (non-Jewish) rulers and nations would hold political sway over the people of Israel and her land. For Israel, this would mean a period of oppression and misery. She would no longer enjoy the freedom that was hers according to God's promises. However, her liberty and restoration would come with the return of the Messiah.

God promised David that he would have a son who would reign over Israel forever (2 Sam 7:11-16). The prophets gave many details of His life. When He came He would bring the Messianic Reign of Peace with Him, and then Israel would enter her divinely appointed role in earnest.

During this period, the Times of the Gentiles would draw to a close and everything would be perfectly restored to its correct position again, by God. The people, the land, their liberty and their assignment would be in their perfect, God-given order.

God showed Daniel all these future events through prophetic messages, dreams and visions. The first of these visions was the interpretation of a dream given to King Nebuchadnezzar (Dan 2). God told Daniel that the dream concerned the Gentile empires, which would control the earth until God Himself would come and take dominion.

We must remember that Israel is forever associated with God and His promises to her. Without God or His promises, and without the covenants or the land, the people would have no future. They would be doomed to assimilation and disappear from the scene of world history forever. But instead, because of God, their future is gloriously bright.

Present world powers may use their influence throughout the earth, yet theirs is only a temporary authority and they will pass away. But Israel, as a nation, will remain and once more be exalted to her former position.

Four Gentile Empires
and an Everlasting Reign of Peace

Daniel's interpretation of King Nebuchadnezzar's dream is a prophecy about four world powers that span the centuries until the final restoration of Israel.

In the dream, God showed the king a statue, *The head of the statue was made of pure gold, its chest and arms of silver, its belly and thighs of bronze, its legs of iron, its feet partly of iron and partly of baked clay* (Dan 2:32-33). The four different metals represent the four Gentile empires that will rule until God takes over (Dan 2:39-40).

Nebuchadnezzar then saw the statue struck and smashed by a rock, which afterwards grew into a mountain and filled the earth:

> While you were watching, a rock was cut out, but not by human hands. It struck the statue on its feet of iron and clay and smashed them. Then the iron, the clay, the bronze, the silver and the gold were broken to pieces at the same time and became like chaff on a threshing floor in the summer. The wind swept them away without leaving a trace. But the rock that struck the statue became a huge mountain and filled the whole earth (Dan 2:34-35).

This stone represents a fifth kingdom, where God Himself is in power and His chosen people reign with Him.

> In the time of those kings, the God of heaven will set up a kingdom that will never be destroyed, nor will it be left to another people. It will crush all those kingdoms and bring them to an end, but it will itself endure forever (Dan 2:44).

Some years later, Daniel himself received a dream (Dan 7). It again depicted the four Gentile empires but, on this occasion, not their outward power and glory as in Nebuchadnezzar's dream of the statue. This time the inner, bestial, nature of each was described:

The first was like a lion, and it had the wings of an eagle. I watched until its wings were torn off and it was lifted from the ground so that it stood on two feet like a man, and the heart of a man was given to it (Dan 7:4).

Following this, Daniel saw a bear with three ribs in its jaws, *And there before me was a second beast, which looked like a bear. It was raised up on one of its sides, and it had three ribs in its mouth between its teeth. It was told, Get up and eat your fill of flesh!* (Dan 7:5).

Thirdly, he saw a leopard with four heads, *After that, I looked, and there before me was another beast, one that looked like a leopard. And on its back it had four wings like those of a bird. This beast had four heads, and it was given authority to rule* (Dan 7:6).

Finally, *After that, in my vision at night I looked, and there before me was a fourth beast terrifying and frightening and very powerful. It had large iron teeth; it crushed and devoured its victims and trampled underfoot whatever was left. It was different from all the former beasts, and it had ten horns* (Dan 7:7).

After the appearance of the fourth beast, Daniel saw how God overthrew and judged it (vv. 9-11). He also saw *one like a son of man, coming in the clouds of heaven. He approached the Ancient of Days and was led into his presence. He was given authority, glory and sovereign power; all peoples, nations and men of every language worshiped him. His dominion is an everlasting dominion that will not pass away, and his kingdom is one that will never be destroyed* (Dan 7:13-14).

Nimrod and the Global Revolt

Neither Jewish scribes nor Christian theologians have ever doubted who this Son of Man is. He is the Messiah. This means that at the climax of the ages, God will take away the power from the Gentile empires and give it to His Messiah, who will then set up the kingdom of God.

The Gentile kingdoms of which Daniel prophesied are ones that have used their power to glorify themselves. They have praised and idolized themselves, oppressed and enslaved others and extended their authority over other nations by means of war and violence. In their pomp and pride they have never given God the glory, nor have they attended to the needs of the people under them.

On the contrary, they have acted on the same principles as Nimrod in Genesis 10:8-12 and 11:1-9. Nimrod was the first person to set up an empire on earth, building it according to the principles described in Genesis 11:4. It consisted of: **a)** Competing with God. **b)** Making a name for himself instead of honoring God. **c)** Ruling by fear instead of by faith and trust. **d)** Deliberately altering God's laws and commandments.

God had originally told man to spread into all the earth and fill it. Instead, these people huddled into a group. This short verse (Gen 11:4) contains the seed-idea at the root of every empire. The principles on which empires are built: ambition, self-exaltation, revolt, fear, dominance and the setting aside of God's law and order.

When a nation, or empire, keeps within the God-given guidelines for law and order, as revealed in the Ten Commandments and the human conscience, God's blessing will rest upon it.

But if a nation perverts justice, sets righteousness aside, opposes the truth and oppresses the people, then the land and its form of leadership will become increasingly demonized. The state will become a ready instrument for insurrection against God. It can last for a time, but eventually it will collapse.

The kingdoms Daniel saw in his dreams and visions were actual, historical kingdoms. He said that the golden head on the statue in Nebuchadnezzar's dream was Nebuchadnezzar himself and his Babylonian kingdom.

> In your hands he has placed mankind and the beasts of the field and the birds of the air. Wherever they live, he has made you ruler over them all. You are that head of gold (Dan 2:38).

We see, then, that this is not a question of mythological imagery, but of historical fact.

The four world empires that Daniel saw, contained all the rebellion and self-aggrandizement which, in embryonic-form, are foretold by Nimrod's kingdom; that is, the collective revolt of mankind against God.

As one kingdom succeeded another, conditions deteriorated and became so uncivilized that they finally took the form of a kingdom worse than all those before it (Dan 7:7). However, after the judgment of that kingdom, God will take control and restore law and order once more. Then a righteous king will arise, Messiah, the Son of Man!

The Reign of Messiah

To the Jews, it was self-evident that the Son of Man mentioned in the book of Daniel was Messiah, the son of David. The son of David would be the king of Israel, and in the Messianic reign the Jews would take up their God-given assignment in earnest.

Isaiah 11:1-10 describes that Messiah. He would be a shoot from the stump of Jesse, a descendant of David. The Spirit of the Lord would rest on Him in full measure:

> The Spirit of wisdom and understanding, the Spirit of counsel and power, the Spirit of knowledge and of the fear of the Lord.... With righteousness he will judge the needy, with justice he will give decisions for the poor of the earth. He will strike the earth with the rod of his mouth; with the breath of his lips he will slay the wicked.... The wolf will live with the lamb, the leopard will lie down with the goat.... They will neither harm nor destroy on all my holy mountain, for the earth will be full of the knowledge of the Lord as the waters cover the sea. *In that day* the Root of Jesse will stand as a banner for the peoples; the nations will rally to him, and his place of rest will be glorious (Isa 11:2,4,6, 9-10).

Isaiah prophesied how Messiah, the Root of Jesse, a son of David, would rule and reign with righteousness in the approaching kingdom of God. This is identified as the fifth kingdom in Nebuchadnezzar's dream. It is the rock that pulverized the idol-statue (the four other kingdoms), and then filled the earth.

Earlier, Isaiah had described the Messiah's reign in His kingdom:

> For to us a child is born, to us a son is given, and *the government will be on his shoulders*. And he will

be called Wonderful Counselor, Mighty God, Everlasting Father, Prince of Peace. *Of the increase of his government and peace there will be no end. He will reign on David's throne and over his kingdom,* establishing and upholding it with justice and righteousness from that time on and forever. The zeal of the Lord Almighty will accomplish this (Isa 9:6-7).

The Seventy Sevens

However, the Times of the Gentiles would continue, until God sent the Messiah to set up His kingdom. One Gentile power would succeed another. All who had insight into prophecy wondered how long this period would be. When would the Messiah come? The answer is given in Daniel 9. Here, we read that Daniel was visited by the Angel Gabriel, who gave him a time plan for the future.

Seventy sevens are decreed for your people and your holy city to finish transgression, to put an end to sin, to atone for wickedness, to bring in everlasting righteousness, to seal up vision and prophecy and to anoint the most holy. Know and understand this: From the issuing of the decree to restore and rebuild Jerusalem until the Anointed One, the ruler, comes, there will be *seven sevens* (weeks), and *sixty-two sevens*. It will be rebuilt with streets and a trench, but in times of trouble. After the sixty-two sevens, the Anointed One will be cut off and will have nothing. The people of the ruler who will come will destroy the city and the sanctuary. The end will come like a flood: War will continue until the end, and desolations have been decreed. He will confirm a covenant with many for one seven, but in the middle of that seven he will put an end to sacrifice and offering. And one who causes desolation will place abominations on a wing of the temple, until the end that is decreed is poured out on him (Dan 9:24-27).

In these scriptures, we read of seventy sevens that is decreed for your people and for your holy city. The people he is talking about are the people of Israel, and the city is Jerusalem. The seventy sevens are seventy units of seven years, 490 years. They were to begin *from the issuing of the decree to restore and rebuild Jerusalem.*

In Daniel's time, during the captivity in Babylon, the people waited for three things: 1) The return to their land (the regathering of the nation), 2) The rebuilding of Jerusalem and the temple, and 3) The coming of Messiah and His kingdom. It was during this period of expectancy that God indicated to Daniel a time plan of 490 years, beginning with the order to rebuild Jerusalem.

The first order was given by Cyrus (Ezra 1:1-4).

> This is what Cyrus king of Persia says: The Lord, the God of heaven, has given me all the kingdoms of the earth and he has appointed me to build a temple for him at Jerusalem in Judah (Ezra 1:2).

This order was given after 70 years of captivity in Babylon, exactly as Jeremiah had prophesied:

> This is what the Lord says: When seventy years are completed for Babylon, I will come to you and fulfill my gracious promise to bring you back to this place (Jer 29:10).

Later, King Artaxerxes gave the command to reconstruct Jerusalem (Neh 1 and 2). This happened in the month, Nisan, in the twentieth year of his reign, the 14th of March, 445 BC. Daniel then speaks of the rebuilding of the city during a period of seven sevens and sixty-two sevens of years (totaling 69 sevens of years, 483 years). After these 483 years, an Anointed person would be *cut off,* or killed (Dan 9:26).

Following that, the city and the temple would be destroyed again, this time by *the people of the ruler* (v. 26). Notice that the stress at this point lies on *the people,* not on the ruler. The *ruler* is emphasized later, as he makes a pact with Israel for the seventieth period of seven; that is to say, for a period of seven years (Dan 9:27).

However, the pact is violated when he stops sacrifice and offering, after half the agreed time. Then, at the end of the seven year period, this leader, who sets up something called *an abomination that causes desolation* (see Dan 11:31-32) is judged and sentenced, as God comes to set up His kingdom once more.

Such details are significant, because God revealed through Daniel what would take place in the future of Israel.

First, Israel will function in the role God intended her to have when He sets up His kingdom again. The Messiah, the Son of Man and the Son of David will be king of all the earth and, above all, king of His chosen people. From Him and His people, the law will go out from Zion.

> In the last days the mountain of the Lord's temple will be established as chief among the mountains; it will be raised above the hills, and all nations will stream to it. Many peoples will come and say, Come, let us go up to the mountain of the Lord, to the house of the God of Jacob. He will teach us his ways, so that we walk in his paths. The law will go out from Zion, the word of the Lord from Jerusalem. He will judge between the nations and will settle disputes for

many peoples. They will beat their swords into plowshares and their spears into pruning hooks. Nation will not take the sword against nation, nor will they train for war anymore (Isa 2:2-4).

Second, various world powers will rise, but all of them will eventually fall.

Third, the period of 483 years in which Jerusalem and the temple are rebuilt, will be followed by their destruction again! This happened in AD 70 It was a terrible tragedy for the Jews to have to leave their land again. Throughout this time, they had not enjoyed autonomy except for a short period under the Macabees.*

But, just as Jeremiah had prophesied (Jer 29:10), after exactly 70 years of captivity in Babylon, the Jews had returned to the land. However, it was not the same as before. The Times of the Gentiles, Gentile domination of Israel's land and people, had begun 70 years earlier, concurrently with the captivity.

With the destruction of Jerusalem in AD 70, only one seven remained. Sixty-nine of them had now passed.

The Visions of Daniel in Historical Perspective

The statue that Nebuchadnezzar saw in his dream symbolized a succession of four heathen empires, which would rule Israel until the return of their Messiah in the clouds of heaven. Daniel 7:13-14 tells us that the Messiah will be given authority and

---

* The Jewish liberation movement that attained political independence for a short period before the Romans took the land.

dominion, and that it will never be taken away from Him:

> In my vision at night I looked, and there before me was one like a son of man, coming with the clouds of heaven. He approached the Ancient of Days and was led into his presence. He was given authority, glory and sovereign power; all peoples, nations and men of every language worshiped him. His dominion is an everlasting dominion that will not pass away, and his kingdom is one that will never be destroyed.

An angel then explained to Daniel, *The four great beasts are four kingdoms that will rise from the earth. But the saints of the Most High will receive the kingdom and will possess it forever—yes, for ever and ever* (Dan 7:17-18).

After the Babylonian Empire, symbolized in Daniel 7:4 by the lion and in Daniel 2:38 by the golden head, came the Medo-Persian Empire, which was indicated by the bear (Dan 7:5) and the chest and arms of silver (Dan 2:32). Following this, the Greek (Hellenistic) Empire arose, represented by the leopard with the four heads (this empire divided into four kingdoms after the death of Alexander the Great) and the belly and thighs of copper (Dan 7:6, 2:32).

Last of all, Daniel 7:7-8 describes an empire symbolized by a different and terrible wild beast which had ten horns:

> After that, in my vision at night I looked, and there before me was a fourth beast terrifying and frightening and very powerful. It had large iron teeth; it crushed and devoured its victims and trampled underfoot whatever was left. It was different from all the former beasts, and it had ten horns. While I was thinking about the horns, there before me was another horn,

a little one, which came up among them; and three of the first horns were uprooted before it. This horn had eyes like the eyes of a man and a mouth that spoke boastfully.

In the statue that Nebuchadnezzar saw, this empire represented by the wild beast is equivalent to the legs and feet that were partly of iron and partly of baked clay (Dan 2:33). The feet naturally had ten toes. This wild animal is the fourth empire, the Roman Empire.

The Roman Empire

The above mentioned kingdoms would follow one another in immediate succession, and the Roman Empire would be the last. Rome was also the most dreadful. It advanced by its unrivalled brutality and aggression. It crushed everything in its path and suppressed the entire then known world.

When, at the end of the 483 years prophesied in Daniel, we come to the time of Jesus and the destruction of the second temple, Rome is in power.

Some have tried to interpret the fourth beast in the vision as the Greek, Hellenistic Empire, with reference to its ten kings. But such a rationalization is made simply to avoid connecting Rome with today's situation. Its advocates simply do not wish to see the parallel in our time, and to accept that the re-emergence of the Roman Empire is foretold in prophecy.

The leopard with the four heads was Greece and its four generals who took over after the death of Alexander. Alexander's kingdom was divided into four parts which, were swallowed up by the next great world power to come, the Roman empire.

The Book of Revelation has several interesting observations to make concerning the fourth wild beast and final kingdom. In Revelation 13:1-2 we read:

> And I saw a beast coming out of the sea. He had ten horns and seven heads, with ten crowns on his horns, and on each head a blasphemous name. The beast I saw resembled a leopard, but had feet like those of a bear and a mouth like that of a lion. The dragon gave the beast his power and his throne and great authority.

Here we read of a beast with the same number of horns, ten. It has similar characteristics to the four beasts in Daniel 7: the lion, the bear, the leopard and the wild beast without a name. This will be the last kingdom, because the Son of Man will come and bring it to trial.

> I looked, and there before me was a white cloud, and seated on the cloud was one like a son of man with a crown of gold on his head and a sharp sickle in his hand (Rev 14:14).

Revelation 17:8 tells us more about this beast. *The beast, which you saw, once was, now is not, and will come up out of the Abyss....* This speaks of a revived empire. In Daniel 9:26 we read that *The people of the ruler who will come will destroy the city and the sanctuary.* Since it was the fourth, or Roman empire that destroyed Jerusalem with its temple, this description fits well.

However, according to history, the Roman Empire slowly declined and therefore it is still to receive its final judgment. Certain elements from within it are latent in the religious, political and judicial systems of modern European civilization.

Toward the end of the age, it is prophesied that these elements will be gathered together to reappear in a revived Roman Empire. It will be a federation of ten states, as symbolized by the ten toes in the statue that Nebuchadnezzar saw. This is the kingdom which the rock will smash, that the Lord will judge. These events are located in the seventieth seven and will take place in the last days.

The Final Seven

At this point the narrative in the book of Daniel changes to describe the ruler, rather than his subjects, the Romans (Dan 9:26-27). This ruler will make a pact or covenant for a period of seven years, after which the final judgment will fall.

As we have seen, at the end of the 483 years, which brought us up to the time of the destruction of the temple, one period of seven remained. This period of seven is concerned with the ruler of the fourth kingdom, and it is these seven years that the book of Revelation describes in detail. However, the book of Revelation locates them in the distant future, at the end of time.

Between the 69th and 70th periods of seven years we find a gap of some two thousand years! Such perspectives are not unusual in prophecies. After God has spoken through His prophets, thousands of years may elapse before their words are fulfilled. Nevertheless, events always take place exactly as God has said. During this particular time lapse two events are taking place, one of which is the worldwide diaspora.

The destruction of the temple was a disaster. God had promised that His kingdom would come after the fourth Gentile empire, but instead we find a massive dispersion of the people. As we saw earlier, this diaspora led to the scattering of the Jewish people to every nation on earth.

Moses had once prophesied future dispersion among many nations (Deut 30:1-4), as had Jeremiah, but this particular dispersion is different from that of the Babylonian captivity. Then, most of the people were taken away to one land. However, in this later dispersion, they are banished to the most distant land under the heavens.

Nonetheless, God had promised:

> Even if you have been banished to the most distant land under the heavens, from there the Lord your God will gather you and bring you back. He will bring you to the land that belonged to your fathers, and you will take possession of it. He will make you more prosperous and numerous than your fathers (Deut 30:4-5).

The Dispersion, A Parenthesis

The nation of Israel will be reassembled because the Lord promised in Daniel 9:24 that *seventy sevens are decreed for your people and your holy city...to seal up vision and prophecy and to anoint the most holy.*

This means that one period of seven years has been kept back until the future. Sixty-nine sevens had passed at the event of the dispersion. The seventieth seven will come at the close of the Gentile Age. After that, the Messiah will return! Then Israel will enter her calling for her land, her people and her city!

The great dispersion, then, is simply a great parenthesis! Humanly speaking it looked as though the end of the Jewish nation had come. But Israel is very much alive and well! Everywhere the people read their prayers and greet one another at Pesach, that is, at Passover or Easter, with the words, Next year in Jerusalem! They mourn for their temple, they long for their city and desire to return to their land, if only to die there.

As previously noted, two events took place during the two thousand year time lapse between the 69th and 70th seven. If the dispersion was one of these great events, then the birth of the Church was the other.

When the Christian church lived in revival, it spread the faith of the Bible, obedience to its Ten Commandments and the practice of biblical ethics, throughout the heathen world. The God of Abraham, Isaac and Jacob was made known to all the Gentile nations by the Church. Where the Church lived in revival, not only was respect for the Jewish people kept alive, but also all that God had said about them in His Word.

However, where the Church lived in pride and apostasy, anti-Semitism and all kinds of religious superstitions abounded.

The Bible makes it plain that the period of Gentile rule will come to an end. This will create several startling changes. Long ago, when Jewish Christians (Jews who saw Jesus as their Messiah) heard that they were to go to the Gentiles with the Gospel, they were shocked and bewildered. A similar turn of events awaits Gentile Christians, non-Jewish believers.

In the last days, God will call His people, Israel, home in earnest. He will restore their fortunes and set them in their predetermined position and role for the next age, The Millennium.

What the Prophets Say
About the Restoration of Israel

Ezekiel clearly prophesied what would happen to the Jewish people. He outlined God's restoration program at the end of the age, which we call the Times of the Gentiles:

> For I will take you out of the nations; I will gather you from all the countries and bring you back into your own land. I will sprinkle clean water on you, and you will be clean; I will cleanse you from all your impurities and from all your idols. I will give you a new heart and put a new spirit in you; I will remove from you your heart of stone and give you a heart of flesh. And I will put my Spirit in you and move you to follow my decrees and be careful to keep my laws. You will live in the land I gave your forefathers; you will be my people, and I will be your God. I will save you from all your uncleanness. I will call for the grain and make it plentiful and will not bring famine upon you. I will increase the fruit of the trees and the crops of the field, so that you will no longer suffer disgrace among the nations because of famine. Then you will remember your evil ways and wicked deeds, and you will loathe yourselves for your sins and detestable practices (Ezek 36:24-31).

God's plan includes the following points:

1. God will gather the Jewish people from every nation to their own land (v. 24).

2. Once there, He will sprinkle clean water on them and cleanse them from all their idols, which they adopted while living among the Gentiles. Materialism, atheism etc, are but some of the "idolatrous isms" and mental strongholds that will fall when the Lord sprinkles His people with the water of purification (v. 25).

3. God will exchange their heart of stone for a soft heart of flesh. All the bitterness and disappointment, inflicted by the Gentiles, will disappear. Their hard hearts will be replaced by hearts that are tender toward God and man. Only God can perform such a miracle (v. 26).

4. God Himself will put His Spirit in their heart and move them to keep His commandments. The same Spirit who inspired Moses to give the Torah to the people will be poured out upon them. He will give them inner power and vitality to truly love the Lord from their heart, and to keep His commandments (v. 27).

The prophet Joel also spoke of this event:

> Then you will know that I am in Israel, that I am the Lord your God, and that there is no other; never again will my people be shamed. And afterward, I will pour out my Spirit on all people. Your sons and daughters will prophesy, your old men will dream dreams, your young men will see visions. Even on my servants, both men and women, I will pour out my Spirit in those days. I will show wonders in the heavens and on the earth, blood and fire and billows of smoke. The sun will be turned to darkness and the moon to blood before the coming of the great and dreadful day of the Lord. And everyone who calls on the name of the Lord will be saved; for on Mount Zion and in Jerusalem there will be deliverance, as the Lord has said, among the survivors whom the Lord calls (Joel 2:27-32).

God's Word will be Literally Fulfilled

On the Day of Pentecost, Peter quotes Joel's words and he applies them to *everyone,* to all nations. But at the end of this age, the original word will be literally fulfilled exactly as the prophet said, *on Mount Zion and in Jerusalem.* And *You will know that I am the Lord your God, and that there is no other; never again will* **my people** *be shamed* (Joel 2:27).

God's Spirit will be poured out on His chosen people *in those days and at that time, when I restore the fortunes of Judah and Jerusalem* (Joel 3:1-2). When that happens, according to the prophet Joel, judgment will be passed on all Gentile nations.

5. *You will live in the land I gave your forefathers; you will be my people, and I will be your God.* When God's plan of restoration is fully realized among the Jewish people, they will settle forever in their land and meet their true destiny. They will become an entire nation, wholeheartedly serving the Lord (Ezek 36:28).

6. God promises to save them and bless them. No longer will they *suffer disgrace among the nations because of famine* but *the fruit of the trees and the crops of the field* will be plenteous. This means that the real place of blessing, prosperity and harmony for the people of Israel is in the land. However, the nation will return to more than just her land: she will return to her God! (Ezek 36:29-30).

7. A fresh revival and perception of God will result. The people will be conscience-stricken and feel ashamed. They will seek their God and loathe themselves for their sins and transgressions. At the same time, a mighty wave of cleansing and holiness will wash over them; bringing restoration, blessing and prosperity (Ezek 36:31-32).

The outpouring of the Holy Spirit, which is prophesied by Joel and Ezekiel, is also foretold by Zechariah:

> And I will pour out on the house of David and the
> inhabitants of Jerusalem a spirit of grace and
> supplication. They will look on me, the one they have
> pierced, and they will mourn for him as one mourns
> for an only child, and grieve bitterly for him as one
> grieves for a firstborn son (Zech 12:10).

When Jerusalem is under extreme pressure, God
will visit his people and pour out His Spirit upon
them.

The prophet Ezekiel describes how the Spirit of
the Lord blew upon dead, dry bones (Ezek 37:4-5,
9-11). The Lord told Ezekiel to prophesy to those
bones that he saw lying there, and then call on the
Spirit to come from the four winds and blow upon
them, so that they would come back to life again.
As a result, a great army consisting of the formerly
dry bones rose and stood to its feet.

> Then you, my people, will know that I am the Lord,
> when I open your graves and bring you up from them.
> I will put my Spirit in you and you will live, and I
> will settle you in your own land. Then you will know
> that I the Lord have spoken, and I have done it,
> declares the Lord (Ezek 37:13-14).

Response to the Calling Still Awaits

The Lord constantly speaks of a regathering and a
filling with the Spirit in the last days. But neither
the regathering, nor the sprinkling with clean water
(the outpouring of the Spirit on the people), will
take place without problems.

The Jews are constantly challenged about their
land and there is increased outside resistance. From
within, there is equally a growing resistance that
says, Leave us alone and let us live in peace like
everyone else. We're the same as every other nation

and we want to live like them. But the Jewish people are not like other people. God Himself said, *A people dwelling alone, Not reckoning itself among the nations* (Num 23:9, NKJV).

God's calling and election has made the Jewish people unique.

> But you, O Israel, *my* servant, Jacob, whom I have chosen, you descendants of Abraham my friend, I took you from the ends of the earth, from its farthest corners I called you. I said you are my *servant;* I have *chosen you* and have *not rejected you* (Isa 41:8-9).

Now when God calls, there must be a response, but if there is no response, problems will arise. Therefore, it is not primarily the right to the land or to be a nation which is the driving force that motivates the Jewish people, but the right to respond to God's eternal call.

He calls the Jews to belong to Him and serve Him. Everything that God does for His people in the last days, the days when the regathering of His people begins in earnest, will lead to one thing, ...*you will be my people, and I will be your God* (Ezek 36:28).

Secularization, relativism, elimination of values and materialism present great perils to the Jewish people. They draw them away from God and cause them to be indifferent to His presence, His word and His calling. Nevertheless, just as their regathering is now underway and heading toward its literal, prophesied fulfillment, so will every other prophetic word of God be fulfilled, including, *I will put my Spirit in you* (Ezek 36:27).

7

Jerusalem, Jerusalem!

Jerusalem is unlike any other city on earth. No city has ever been so visited, admired, hated, celebrated or mourned over as Jerusalem. It has a central place in several religions, and arouses feelings in the hearts of millions of people. No city in the world has as many foreign correspondents as Jerusalem. It seems as if they are expecting some very important event to take place there!

When simply visiting Jerusalem something happens to you. Even the most stoic, the most blase or the most critical person, cannot leave the city without being changed and affected by it.

Behind its stone facades, beneath its huge masonry blocks, something eternal is present. Something timeless fills the atmosphere, pervading everything and affecting everyone. The city is tarrying, her stones are waiting. Jerusalem's destiny is ordained of old. For centuries, heathen nations have vainly attempted to overthrow and desecrate her. But she stands firm as ever, having not yet entered the full realization of what she is destined to be.

City of the Future

Visiting Jerusalem, it is easy for one's attention to be caught up with all the religious trappings and commerce surrounding holy places, holy stones and holy crosses. But behind these lies something very

different. Within her people is a genuine longing
and desire for their city to fulfill her calling.

Jerusalem's greatness does not lie in the past,
though she can boast a history like no other city
on earth. Her greatness lies in the future, and her
future is closer than ever! It is as though an unseen
veil is about to be taken away, thus revealing
Jerusalem's glory and appointed end. Her entire
atmosphere breathes hope and a confident expecta-
tion of something good to come.

However, at the same time, one can sense more
strongly than ever the presence of religious and
rebellious spirits, spirits of animosity and of violence.
Opposition to Jerusalem becoming a footstool for the
Great King grows, as the time for His coming draws
near.

Though Jerusalem's future is so tremendously
bright, we must also know that her history can be
traced back to ancient times. Significantly, she first
appears in Scripture after Abram's victory over the
mightiest powers of his day (Gen 14:1-20). Abram
had liberated Lot and was on his way home, when
he was met by Priest-King Melchizedek.

Melchizedek, who was King of Salem, invited him
to eat bread and drink wine, and then blessed him.
Following this, Abram gave Melchizedek a tenth of
the spoils of war.

> After Abram returned from defeating Kedorlaomer and
> the kings allied with him, the king of Sodom came
> out to meet him in the Valley of Shaveh (that is, the
> King's Valley). Then Melchizedek king of Salem
> brought out bread and wine. He was priest of God
> Most High, and he blessed Abram, saying, Blessed be
> Abram by God Most High, Creator of heaven and

earth. And blessed be God Most High, who delivered your enemies into your hand (Gen 14:17-20).

Salem is the same as Jerusalem. Later Abraham returned there, to the land of Moriah, because that was where God told him to sacrifice his son Isaac (Gen 22). On Mount Moriah the Lord appeared to him. *Do not lay a hand on the boy, he said. Do not do anything to him. Now I know that you fear God, because you have not withheld from me your son, your only son* (Gen 22:12).

Verse 14 continues: *And Abraham called the name of that place (Jehovah-jireh)* **The-Lord-Will-Provide**: *as it is said to this day,* **In the mount of the Lord it shall be provided** (NKJV). This Mount of the Lord, on which the Scriptures say something will be seen, later became the site of the temple, Temple Mount.

City of David

After Abraham's time, the city appears under the name of Jebus, and in the hands of the Jebusites. The children of Israel had not managed to take possession of it, though the city lay within the limits of Canaan. However, David sent Joab, his commander-in-chief, there and the city was successfully taken.

David then made Jerusalem the capital of Israel and reigned there for thirty-three years. It is significant that David was the first king of Israel to reign from Jerusalem; because one day, Messiah, the Son of David will also rule from there.

Through the years, it was always in David's heart to build a temple in Jerusalem for his Lord, but God told him that his son was to do it instead (2 Sam 7:8-16). Realizing he was not going to receive permission to build, David did everything in his power to prepare for the temple, so his son Solomon could erect it as soon as he was old enough. He also bought Ornan's threshing floor, which later became the temple site (1 Chron 21:24).

For a long time, God had spoken about a place for His Name to be. He had talked to Moses about it, and He also spoke to David:

> Since the day I brought my people out of Egypt, I have not chosen a city in any tribe of Israel to have a temple built for my Name to be there, nor have I chosen anyone to be the leader over my people Israel. *But now I have chosen Jerusalem for my Name to be there,* and I have chosen David to rule my people Israel (2 Chron 6:5-6).

City of Festivals

So it was that God associated His presence with Jerusalem and the temple there. His people were to make pilgrimages to Jerusalem three times a year, following the Law of Moses. There, in the Temple they would celebrate Pesach—Passover (Easter), Shavout—Pentecost (Whitsun) and Succoth—the Feast of Tabernacles.

The temple, the reading of the Law, the sacrifices and the keeping of the festivals were to be a picture to Israel. They were a prophetic preview of God Himself, His attributes and His plan of redemption. By these means, God was teaching His people about salvation. This was why He was so concerned that the festivals should be kept at the proper time, in the proper place and in the proper manner, and that the heart of them all should be in Jerusalem.

One cannot understand the spiritual significance the Jews place on Jerusalem without realizing that it is inextricably connected with their longing for God and His commands to them, to worship and praise Him there.

Today, people say that Jerusalem is the city of three religions: Judaism, Christianity and Islam. The inference is that these three groups should divide the city into three more or less equal parts, and then all live there happily ever after. But Jerusalem is not the city of three religions. Jerusalem is the City of God, and the place from where He has chosen to reveal Himself to His people and the rest of the world.

This is why Isaiah says:

> In the last days the mountain of the Lord's temple will be established as chief among the mountains; it will be raised above the hills, and all nations will stream to it. Many peoples will come and say, Come, let us go up to the mountain of the Lord, to the house of the God of Jacob. He will teach us his ways, so that we may walk in his paths. *The law will go out from Zion, the word of the Lord from Jerusalem* (Isa 2:2-3).

Isaiah 25:7 continues, *On this mountain he will destroy the shroud that enfolds all peoples, the sheet that covers all nations.*

The City of God

The more one reads the Bible, the more one realizes the significance of Jerusalem. The Lord has associated His presence with her in a very special way. In the same way that God speaks of an everlasting covenant with Abraham, He also speaks of an everlasting relationship with Jerusalem. When prophets prophesy over Jerusalem, it is always with a bright future for her.

Other cities have exerted greater political, cultural and economic influence, yet they disappeared from world affairs centuries ago and today they are totally insignificant. But Jerusalem is still here.

The city has known times of glory, and also periods of decadence, oppression, plunder and devastation. However, she has always risen to her feet again, and in spite of it all she is standing today.

Even when the Romans destroyed the city, plowed up her ground, changed her name to Aelia Capitolina and barred the Jews from living there, Jerusalem survived—and it was not long before her people were back again. The Jews have always lived there, even when Jerusalem was at her lowest, because she belongs to them. She is given to them by God.

It is not just the various events in Jerusalem's history that are precious to the Jews, but the city itself, because God has chosen it. Psalm 48 describes Jerusalem as: *the city of our God,* and *his holy mountain* (v. 1). Mount Zion is called *the joy of the whole earth*, and Jerusalem, *the city of the Great King* (v. 2). It is said of her: *the city of the Lord Almighty,* and *God makes her secure forever* (v. 8).

Psalm 50:2 says, *From Zion, perfect in beauty, God shines forth.*

Psalm 87:1-3 declares, ***He has set his foundation*** *on the holy mountain;* ***the Lord loves the gates of Zion*** *more than all the dwellings of Jacob. Glorious things are said of you,* ***O city of God***.

The Lord loves Jerusalem and is so involved in her future that He is with her all the time, holding her up and never letting her fall. He says of her in

Isaiah 49:16, *See, I have engraved you on the palms of my hands; your walls are ever before me.*

God is so concerned for her welfare and the fulfillment of His plans for her, that He says:

> For Zion's sake I will not keep silent, for Jerusalem's sake I will not remain quiet, till her righteousness shines out like the dawn, her salvation like a blazing torch. The nations will see your righteousness, and all kings your glory; you will be called by a new name that the mouth of the Lord will bestow. You will be a crown of splendor in the Lord's hand, a royal diadem in the hand of your God. No longer will they call you Deserted, or name your land Desolate. But you will be called Hephzibah, and your land Beulah; for the Lord will take delight in you, and your land will be married. As a young man marries a maiden, so will your sons marry you; as a bridegroom rejoices over his bride, so will your God rejoice over you. I have posted watchmen on your walls, O Jerusalem; they will never be silent day or night. You who call on the Lord, give yourselves no rest, and give him no rest until he establishes Jerusalem and makes her the praise of the earth (Isa 62:1-7).

Furthermore, He promises Jerusalem, ...*you will be called Sought After,* **The City No Longer Deserted** (v. 12).

Even so, the prophets had to constantly reproach Jerusalem. Instead of becoming a place of worship, she has repeatedly become a nest of thieves. Instead of being a place of revelation and glory, she has too often become the scene of misuse of authority, false and flattering prophecies and a dissolute lifestyle.

God is angered with His people when they sin against Him and forsake Him.

In Jeremiah 2:2 He says, *Go and proclaim in the hearing of Jerusalem: I remember the devotion of your youth, how as a bride you loved me and followed me through the desert, through a land not sown.*

He further declares, *My people have committed two sins: They have forsaken me, the spring of living water, and have dug their own cisterns, broken cisterns that cannot hold water* (Jer 2:13).

When God's people left Him, they also left the protection they enjoyed for themselves, their land and their city. The city had been given to them as a national center for the worship and service of God. Consequently, when they strayed from Him they forfeited the privilege of His blessing. Although they continued celebrating their festivals and holidays, they did so in a manner disrespectful to God:

> These people come near to me with their mouth and honor me with their lips, but their hearts are far from me. Their worship of me is made up only of rules taught by men (Isa 29:13).

Furthermore He says, *Stop bringing meaningless offerings! Your incense is detestable to me. New Moons, Sabbaths and convocations—I cannot bear your evil assemblies* (Isa 1:13).

In Isaiah 56:7 the Lord had said of the temple, *...my house will be called a house of prayer.* However, in Jeremiah 7:11 He says in dismay, *Has this house, which bears my Name, become a den of robbers to you? But I have been watching! declares the Lord.*

God longed for a people who were willing to obey Him from their heart. He desired a people who loved Him with all their heart, all their soul and all their strength.

Years earlier He had declared:

> Hear, O Israel: The Lord our God, the Lord is one. Love the Lord your God with all your heart and with

all your soul and with all your strength. These commandments that I give you today are to be upon your hearts (Deut 6:4-6).

However, the people's hearts hardened even more, and their ceremonies degenerated into rituals of mere lip service. There was no heart devotion involved. They insisted on maintaining a pious front and their man-made traditions, while at the same time attempting to keep the God-appointed feasts, to say all the right prayers and keep the correct animal sacrifices. But they lost the whole point.

The true purpose of the festivals—the whole-hearted worship and love of God, a holy lifestyle, love and mercy toward their fellowmen—was all forgotten. In its place was selfishness, greed, indifference and hatred, all camouflaged in a religious exterior of reverence and righteousness. But God, who searches the hearts of men, saw through it all and warned His citizens:

> Take warning, O Jerusalem, or I will turn away from you and make your land desolate so no one can live in it (Jer 6:8).

City of the Prophets

When God issued His warnings He did so through the prophets. Isaiah, Jeremiah, Hosea, Amos and others delivered the word of the Lord directly at the heart of Israel's backslidden behavior.

Because of their stand, the prophets were not exactly voted most popular person in their country. Several of them suffered cruel reprisals but God strengthened them, sometimes enabling them to withstand the whole nation alone (Jer 1:17-19). On occasions, the prophets even had to challenge the entire religious establishment. Jeremiah says:

> From the least to the greatest, all are greedy for gain; prophets and priests alike, all practice deceit. They dress the wound of my people as though it were not serious. Peace, peace, they say, when there is no peace (Jer 6:13-14).

Hosea says something similar, *Don't point your finger at someone else, and try to pass the blame to him! Look, priest, I am pointing my finger at you* (Hos 4:4, TLB). So God was bringing the prophets and priests to trial. But why?

> My people are destroyed from lack of knowledge. Because you have rejected knowledge, I also reject you as my priests; because you have ignored the law of your God, I also will ignore your children (Hos 4:6).

We could go through the words of all the prophets and discover the same thing time and again. The people are in covenant with God. He has made all His blessings available to them. But they can never reap the benefit of these blessings until they give Him their love, follow Him and obey Him with all their hearts.

God longs for a people who will serve Him wholeheartedly. But when callousness, apathy and unfaithfulness are on the rise, the people are on the way down. God says in Hosea 5:4, *Their deeds do not permit them to return to their God. A **spirit of prostitution** (unfaithfulness) is in their heart; they do not acknowledge the Lord.*

God sent prophet after prophet to them, yet the people still did not repent. Finally judgment came. Jerusalem was besieged, overthrown and destroyed. Jeremiah, who had prophesied to the people and warned them of developments, witnessed this tragedy. In his Lamentations over Jerusalem he mourns, crying:

> How deserted lies the city, once so full of people! How like a widow is she, who once was great among the nations! She who was queen among the provinces has now become a slave.... All the splendor has departed from the Daughter of Zion (Lam 1:1,6).

Jerusalem has been through this experience more than other cities. Many have reached out to take her.

However, each time she put her trust in the Lord, as in the days of King Hezekiah (Isa 37), she was shielded supernaturally, even from clearly superior enemies. But if she was unfaithful, she lost her covenant protection; and Jerusalem was overpowered by her foes, taken, plundered and sacked.

An Everlasting City

Since the days of Nebuchadnezzar, many nations have laid siege to Jerusalem. After the Babylonians came the Persians, then the Greeks, the Romans, Byzantines, Muslims, Crusaders, Mamelukes, Ottomans, British and Jordanians.

For centuries, superpowers in every age have grasped at her. They have wanted to own her, use her and destroy her; but notably, every empire that has had designs on Jerusalem has finally fallen, while Jerusalem still stands.

Why is this? The Lord explains why in Zechariah 8:2, *I am very jealous for Zion, I am burning with jealousy for her.* Jerusalem is the apple of His eye, and He who watches over her does not slumber or sleep (Ps 121:4). God does not want her to suffer harm nor will He reject her, because He has fixed the place of His Name and presence in Jerusalem forever.

When His people came under enemy attack, it was because of their backsliding and sin. It was not God's will. That is why He is always ready to regather them, restore them and save them.

> This is what the Lord says: I will return to Zion and dwell in Jerusalem. Then Jerusalem will be called *The City of Truth,* and the mountain of the Lord Almighty will be called The Holy Mountain. This is what the Lord Almighty says: Once again men and women of ripe old age will sit in the streets of Jerusalem, each with cane in hand because of his age (Zech 8:3-4).

God also says, ...Jerusalem will remain intact in her place (Zech 12:6).

A glorious future awaits Jerusalem. It is not the United Nations' plan to make her an international city of three religions under the auspices of the UN. Jerusalem is the City of God, the capital city of Israel and her people, the Jews.

> I am very jealous for Jerusalem and Zion, but I am very angry with the nations that feel secure. I was only a little angry, but they added to the calamity. Therefore, this is what the Lord says: I will return to Jerusalem with mercy, and there my house will be rebuilt. And the measuring line will be stretched out over Jerusalem.... My towns will again overflow with prosperity, and the Lord will again comfort Zion and choose Jerusalem (Zech 1:14-17).

In other words, if any city has a future Jerusalem does. If any city is associated with the Jewish people, Jerusalem is.

When the Romans destroyed her temple in AD 70 it seemed as though everything was lost. After that, she came under the dominion of successive Gentile nations. Jesus spoke of it when He prophesied over Jerusalem, They will fall by the sword and will be taken as prisoners to all the nations. Jerusalem will be trampled on by the Gentiles until the times of the Gentiles are fulfilled (Luke 21:24).

City of the Messiah

Just as the dispersion that Jesus prophesied was fulfilled, so too, the regathering will also be fulfilled, and it has already begun. The time would come, the Bible declared, when Jerusalem would no longer be trampled underfoot by the Gentiles, but would be restored as the capital city of the Jews and of Israel.

When Israel miraculously became a nation again, Jerusalem was divided. East Jerusalem was under Jordanian (Muslim rule) and it was prohibited for a Jew to visit the Western Wall (Wailing Wall) to pray.

Nineteen years later, in 1967, as a result of the Six Day War, Jerusalem was reunited to become one city. Today she is the capital of Israel, and despite rumblings from the Muslim world, Israel will never concede to the demand for a divided Jerusalem again.

As previously mentioned, Muslims regard Jerusalem as a holy city, though without any real support in the Koran. This myth was added later to supply religious motivation for control of the city.

This is the core issue of Muslim aggression toward Israel. The Muslims want to gain political and spiritual control of Jerusalem at all costs. Why? Because Jerusalem has an essential role to play in the future, and Islam, as a rival religion, wants to block it.

Jerusalem is the city of Abraham, David and the prophets. But above all, she is the city of Messiah. It is Jerusalem to which the Messiah will return. He will reign and rule there. Jerusalem would have no special significance apart from the Messiah. It would simply be like any other city and if that were so, then Jerusalem would be nothing more than an interesting museum of three religions.

This is why, when looking at Jerusalem from a merely human point of view, people want to internationalize it, place it under UN jurisdiction, and satisfy the demands of differing religions for their holy places. However, this is neither her purpose nor her destiny.

Jerusalem is the City of the Great King. She is the scene of the climax and end of this age and the inception of the next, The Age of the Messiah. Jerusalem is the center of all true spiritual activity in the world. Rome, London, New York or Los Angeles: none of these is the center, only Jerusalem.

As the Last Days approach, Jerusalem will figure increasingly in the attention and minds of men and women. Already we hear more about the Middle East and Jerusalem than about any other foreign political subject. Every country, and almost every person, has some opinion about Jerusalem. All eyes are turning in her direction.

One day, every eye will be looking toward Jerusalem and the Bible tells us what will happen at that time.

City of Destiny

From AD 70, the year of the destruction of the second temple, until now, God has offered His grace to the heathen world through the preaching of the Gospel.

In the Bible, every period of grace is followed by a period of judgment. God will judge the Gentile nations on how they treated the Jewish people during the time of their dispersion. The scene of this judgment will be Jerusalem.

The time is coming when the Gentile nations will first withdraw their support for Israel, then isolate it and finally launch a concerted attack against it and against Jerusalem. The Gulf War (1991) was a final full-dress rehearsal for such an attack. Would it be possible to unite many nations in a united assault against one target country? Yes, it worked.

Iraq was defeated by a coalition of countries mutually at enmity with one another—Syria and the USA. How did they suddenly become friends? What agreements had they made? Why did they take up the Palestinian question directly after the victory in the Gulf? What demands did the Arabs make concerning Israel before joining with the coalition forces in the Gulf War?

Why were President Bush and his Secretary of State, James Baker, so very anxious in their negotiations to put pressure on Israel to give up the West Bank, and why the blank refusal to give Israel new loan guarantees?

Two things have become noticeable: firstly, there is increased frustration in the USA as Israel refuses to fit into its plans for a New World Order, secondly, the Arab world is putting pressure on the USA to stop her supporting Israel. This can only have one result—the decline of the USA.

No superpower that has turned its back on Israel has ever survived. Britain had its historic chance to bless the Jewish people at the end of the Second World War. It actively opposed Jewish immigration to Israel instead. Those who had survived the hell of the concentration camps were interned in refugee camps on Cyprus, or dragged back to Germany against their will.

When the UN eventually decided to divide the Palestinian Mandate, the British took the side of the Arabs against the Jews. They could not stop the birth of the State of Israel, but they lost their entire empire and ceased being a world power.

The same thing will happen to the USA. Until now, it has supported Israel and been blessed. But Bush and Baker introduced another policy that will have ominous consequences for the USA.

Many Christian pastors and politicians had always been invited to Bush's prayer breakfasts. But his flirtations with the Arab world went so far that he demanded the attendance of at least one Muslim priest as well.

As early as 1981, a prophetic message was given, saying that the man to be voted president of the USA in 1989 would become an enemy of Israel. Then years later, Israel felt a coolness in the USA's attitude toward her, such as she had never felt before.

At the same time, a final practice of all that Zechariah long ago prophesied would happen, was rehearsed nearby. Many nations were gathered against Iraq, but in the future, it will be against Jerusalem.

> I am going to make Jerusalem a cup that sends all the surrounding peoples reeling. Judah will be besieged as well as Jerusalem. On that day, when all the nations of the earth are gathered against her, I will make Jerusalem an immovable rock for all the nations. All who try to move it will injure themselves (Zech 12:2-3).

A Protected City

From these words, we can see that the time is coming when all the nations will gather against Jerusalem. However, they will not succeed. God is shielding and defending Jerusalem—and it is His plans that will succeed.

As hostile attitudes toward her intensify, they will be reflected in a rise of anti-Semitism, and Israel and Jerusalem will become increasingly isolated. Israel's refusal to accept the world's humanistic-political programs and aspirations will cause many countries, such as the USA, to become aggravated and angry toward her.

There are other lands, such as Syria, which would simply like to annihilate Israel, but they lack the political ability to do so. There will be many motives that will cause the nations of the world to converge and unite against Israel. But God's plan is totally different:

> In those days and at that time, when I restore the fortunes of Judah and Jerusalem, I will *gather all nations* and bring them down to the Valley of Jehoshaphat. There I will enter into judgment against them *concerning my inheritance, my people Israel,* for they scattered my people among the nations and divided up my land (Joel 3:1-2).

What looks like a political-military solution to the conflict in the Middle East will finally be revealed to be a judgment upon all nations. When God executes this judgment, the Age of the Gentiles and their power over the land of Israel and the Jewish people, will come to an end.

What will happen then? Zechariah tells us that on that day, the day many prophets spoke about, the day of the Lord's judgment of the nations, the Messiah will stand on the Mount of Olives.

> On that day his feet will stand on the Mount of Olives, east of Jerusalem, and the Mount of Olives will be split in two from east to west, forming a great valley, with half of the mountain moving north and half moving south (Zech 14:4).

Zechariah also tells us that the city of Jerusalem will be changed:

> On that day living water will flow out from Jerusalem, half to the eastern sea (the Dead Sea) and half to the western sea (the Mediterranean), in summer and in winter. The Lord will be king over the whole earth. On that day there will be one Lord, and his name the only name (Zech 14:8-9).

Capital City of the Globe

The time will come when God will reign over the whole earth from its center and capital, Jerusalem. For the Jewish people, the reign of Messiah will mean security and refreshment. *It will be inhabited; never again will it be destroyed. Jerusalem will be secure* (Zech 14:11).

But what will this mean for the Gentiles?

> Then the survivors from all the nations that have attacked Jerusalem will go up year after year to worship the King, the Lord Almighty, and to celebrate the Feast of Tabernacles (Zech 14:16).

Events can be summarized as follows:

1. The nations will attack Jerusalem.
2. With God's help, Jerusalem is defended and the nations defeated.
3. The Messiah returns.
4. The Gentile nations are judged by God.

5. King Messiah reigns in Jerusalem.

6. The house of the Lord, the Temple, is rebuilt (see Zech 14:21; Ezek 40-48).

7. Israel is ordained a nation of priests to God.

8. The nations travel to Jerusalem to pray, worship, celebrate and receive revelation and teaching.

9. Jerusalem becomes the center of world affairs, while the Temple and the Messiah become the focal point of Jerusalem.

Jerusalem! What a future! No other city has been afforded such promises or such a future. Furthermore, the Book of Revelation says that after the Messianic Millennium, Jerusalem will receive a final transformation. Then, God's plan of redemption will be complete and all of God's promises, from those given to Abraham and onwards, will be fulfilled.

> Then I saw a new heaven and a new earth, for the first heaven and the first earth had passed away, and there was no longer any sea. I saw the Holy City, the new Jerusalem, coming down out of heaven from God, prepared as a bride beautifully dressed for her husband (Rev 21:1-2).

A Holy City

This is the heavenly hope—eternity; not just the reign of the Messiah, but the state and condition of eternity. Then, when sin, death, all the attributes of this age and all its works are over; when this old earth with its kingdoms and cities is gone, Jerusalem will remain—but in a new form.

What will the heavenly city be like? Blissful, sublime and surpassing human thought! And those who imagine that the end of the Jewish people is near, are in for a surprise in this heavenly city.

> And he carried me away in the Spirit to a mountain
> great and high, and showed me the Holy City,
> Jerusalem, coming down out of heaven from God. It
> shone with the glory of God, and its brilliance was
> like that of a very precious jewel, like a jasper, clear
> as crystal. It had a great, high wall with twelve gates,
> and with twelve angels at the gates. On the gates
> were written the names of the twelve tribes of Israel
> (Rev 21:10-12).

The Jews will be in heaven too. The names of the
tribal patriarchs are inscribed over the twelve gates
of the new, heavenly Jerusalem. God's nature is
eternal, His plans are eternal, His city is everlasting
and His people are everlasting. *I have loved you
with an everlasting love; I have drawn you with
loving-kindness* (Jer 31:3).

Jerusalem and the Jewish people have an
everlasting, central place in God's worldwide plan
of salvation. They have carried God's revelation
through history, and administered the service in the
Temple. It was the Jews who cared for the Land of
Israel, and Jerusalem is their city. Through them
the Messiah came, the Son of David, the Great King;
and it will be from their city, Jerusalem, that He
will reign in peace and righteousness over the whole
earth.

We will see all the promises concerning Jerusalem
fulfilled. Jerusalem is the part in the picture that
will make it complete, meaningful and beautiful.
Thus, it is not strange that the crowning words of
the prophetic book of Ezekiel are these: *And the
name of the city from that time on will be: The Lord
Is There* (Ezek 48:35).

God Himself, His salvation, His plans and His
glory are tied to Jerusalem forever.

8

Ruth's Decision

Israel is the land of the future and the Jews are the people of the future, not because they are any better than other nations—all are equal before God—but because of the calling God has placed on them. This calling means blessing for every nation but it also provokes resistance, prejudice and evil.

The Land—A Protection for the People

Mankind's worst atrocities have been continually vented upon the Jewish people. They have been scattered, despised refugees without a land. Now the situation has changed. They have Eretz Israel—a land to which they can return.

Just think of the many Jews who have said, If only we'd had a land somewhere, the holocaust could never have happened. The holocaust was a horrifying nightmare, but as a result the State of Israel became a welcome reality. The Jews could then be on their way home again. Therefore, it is obvious that Israel is the best possible protection against anti-Semitism.

However, hostility remains. Anti-Semitism has taken on a new form and become anti-Zionism. Sometimes one can hear anti-Semites say, I have nothing against Jews, but I don't like Israel or Zionism; as if one can treat the people and their land separately. This is impossible because they are inextricably joined together through the promises of

God. Anti-Zionism is merely Anti-Semitism in another guise.

The Promised Land

How should a non-Jew react to Israel and the Jewish people? What should he think and feel about them? Is Israel merely the scene of religious history? Is it only a museum full of holy places for people to visit for a few days of edification? If so, then it makes no difference whether the land belongs to Jordan, whether it is called Palestine or is administrated by the UN. It is no more than the sentimental focal point for different religions.

But this is not so. The land is forever linked to the people, to the promises and to God Himself. All the promises, of which you have read only a fraction in this book, are valid for the future too. The future is most important for both the people and the land. To consider the formation of the State of Israel as just a coincidence, reveals a grave degree of ignorance and unwillingness to understand the prophetic scriptures.

Israel's very existence as a modern nation is a sheer miracle, and the fulfilled prophecies prove the reliability of God's Word. This does not mean that you are to become a palm leaf-waving romantic, almost falling into a trance every time you hear the name Israel or meet a Jew! Many Israel-romantics have been disappointed to discover that Israel is a land like other lands, in that its people have attitudes, problems and difficulties like other peoples.

Today, it is not romanticism and sentimentality that are needed, but a realistic insight into what

Israel is—and as a result, a resolute decision of firm friendship.

For or Against

Israel leaves no one untouched. However secularized people may be, the land of Israel and its people point not only to the existence of God, but also to His plans and promises for the whole of mankind.

There is something inevitable, something convincing about Israel, and there is also something that compels everyone to take a stand. The question is, which stand have you taken?

Throughout the Bible we can read of non-Jews who have blessed Israel. History too, provides many examples. Orde Wingate and Raoul Wallenberg are two of them. However, we are not concerned with heroic figures but with ordinary people and their decisions. Each of us must make a stand, and as time passes the more important and solemn that decision will become.

When Jews were herded off by the thousands to the concentration camps, only a few onlookers were prepared to side with them. The majority dropped their heads or looked away. The philosophy of shame reigned and many went around in silence, their consciences burning. But those who kept quiet and refused to protest were actually taking a stand. No one can remain neutral. Life is not neutral.

Some time ago, a friend of mine met a former SS soldier in Austria. Nervously, he took out photographs of his days as a young private on the eastern front. Apologetic and laden with guilt, he talked about Jew hunts, arrests and executions.

I didn't realize, he explained, I was so very young at the time. Everybody was doing it.

But his life was ruined. Memories have dogged him ever since. He was like a hunted man. He seemed constantly on the watch for people who could relieve him of his memories and tell him everything was all right or that it was all just a bad dream.

In spite of all the words that it will never be repeated, the risk of another holocaust still remains. Madmen deny it, others just forget it. But Arab anti-Semitism is as implacable and unrelenting as ever; while in the West, cool indifference is common. Among Christians, replacement theology with its sometimes hidden, sometimes blatantly open anti-Semitism, is rife in some circles.

Even those who say they bless Israel, display deep ignorance, and sometimes alarming indifference can be found. We have so many other things to think about, they say. There are other things to be involved in too, you know!

But if you want to be blessed, you must bless what God blesses and He is blessing Israel. If you want blessing, you must put first things first—what God puts first. God's priorities are His land, His people and His plan of redemption.

Ruth—An Example

The Book of Ruth describes a non-Jewish woman, a Moabitess. The account begins at a time of widespread famine in Israel. A woman named Naomi had left Bethlehem with her husband and sons, and moved to the land of Moab, to settle there. They had been uprooted and dispersed through drought and famine, just as many thousands of Jews were to be dispersed throughout the world in later years.

During this time, Naomi's sons married Moabite women and her husband died. The family was assimilated, just as many other Jews have been assimilated in the lands of their dispersion in succeeding years. Eventually, Naomi's sons also died, just as many Jews have died, far from Zion, during the centuries of the diaspora.

It was then that Naomi heard that, *The Lord had come to the aid of his people by providing food for them* (Ruth 1:6). Similarly today, many Jews are hearing that God has come to the aid of His people and has begun to regather them.

Naomi decided to return to her own land, to her hometown. Her two daughters-in-law, Ruth and Orpah, accompanied her on the first stretch of the journey. She then gave them the opportunity to return to their native land. Orpah did so, but not Ruth.

> Look, said Naomi, your sister-in-law is going back to her people and her gods. Go back with her. But Ruth replied, Don't urge me to leave you or to turn back from you. Where you go I will go, and where you stay I will stay. Your people will be my people and your God my God. Where you die I will die, and there I will be buried. May the Lord deal with me, be it ever so severely, if anything but death separates you and me (Ruth 1:15-17).

Choose Blessing

This was Ruth's decision, and her choice revealed several facts. Firstly, she realized that Naomi, a Jewess, ought to live in her own land. Secondly, she was aware that the God of Naomi was the Living God, and finally, she realized that Naomi's people were her people.

But Ruth was a Moabitess and not Jewish by birth. As a Moabitess, she was free to make her decision for or against the Jews. She could bless or curse them; support and help them; or remain indifferent, busy with other matters and go her own way. Ruth chose to bless, and was blessed herself. Through her, David was born, a future King of Israel and a type of the Messiah.

Because of her decision, Ruth was given an important place in God's ongoing revelation of Himself. She was a necessary instrument, a part in His overall plan.

However, Ruth could not be a blessing until she had made her choice. She weighed the matter carefully and made her decision. It was thorough and radical. Her decision changed her life, her future, her place and way of living; in fact, everything. It was not a rushed, emotional choice, but one that was based on lifelong devotion.

The same decision is ours today, and that of the Christian Church at large. We stand at the threshold of that decision.

On the one hand, we can choose to go back with Orpah to the influence and spirit of this world with its opinions and attitudes. Unfortunately, some will do it. Their choice will be marked by a growing coolness toward Israel and a ready condoning of anti-Semitism. Finally, they will become religious pawns in the game against Israel and against God.

For our part, we can choose to go the way of Ruth. This implies the realization that the land of Israel belongs to the Jewish people. It means that the God of Abraham, Isaac and Jacob is ours, and that His words and promises in the Bible are of absolute and immediate relevance today. It means that the Church must make the cause of the Jews its own.

Having made that decision, even if some become cooler, distancing themselves and backing down, Israel will still know that she has friends. They will be true friends who will not let her down, manipulate her or have hidden, false motives.

These people will be motivated by God's Word, His promises and by His love that is poured out in their hearts. This love asks for nothing in return and is not scheming or calculating. It is a selfless love, not dependent on a response, but motivated by God's faithfulness to His people and His promises.

When you have made your decision, what is your next step?

a) Pray for the peace of Jerusalem. *Pray for the peace of Jerusalem: May those who love you be secure. May there be peace within your walls and security within your citadels. For the sake of my brothers and friends, I will say, Peace be within you. For the sake of the house of the Lord our God, I will seek your prosperity* (Ps 122:6-9).

b) Bless the seed of Abraham. *I will bless those who bless you, and whoever curses you I will curse; and all peoples on earth will be blessed through you* (Gen 12:3).

c) Comfort, support and encourage the people of God. *Comfort, comfort my people, says your God. Speak tenderly to Jerusalem, and proclaim to her that her hard service has been completed, that her sin has been paid for, that she has received from the Lord's hand double for all her sins* (Isa 40:1-2).

d) Oppose every form of anti-Semitism and anti-Zionism by spreading correct information concerning Israel and the Jewish people. *Do not boast over those branches. If you do, consider this:*

You do not support the root, but the root supports you (Rom 11:18).

e) Support Israel and the regathering of the Jewish people financially. *Surely the islands look to me; in the lead are the ships of Tarshish, bringing your sons from afar, with their silver and gold, to the honor of the Lord your God, the Holy One of Israel, for he has endowed you with splendor. Foreigners will rebuild your walls, and their kings will serve you. Though in anger I struck you, in favor I will show you compassion* (Isa 60:9-10).

Aliens will shepherd your flocks; foreigners will work your fields and vineyards (Isa 61:5).

When the Church recognizes its place in praying for and supporting the Jewish people, God will be given even better conditions for the completion of His work with Israel. However, this will mean a change for the Church, as well as for Israel.

Just as Peter had difficulties understanding that the Gospel should spread to the Gentiles, so too, many Christians will find it hard to understand when the initiative returns to the Jewish people. But whoever listens to the Spirit and searches the Scriptures will see how all things converge and move toward their prophesied end. God's plan for the Jews will be gloriously fulfilled.

Appendix

Important Years in Israel's History

BC

1400–1200	Immigration of the tribes of Israel.
approx. 1000	King Saul's reign.
1004–975	King David's reign.
975–926	King Solomon's reign.
925	The kingdom divides: Israel (north); Judah (south).
722	Israel becomes an Assyrian province.
587	Judah conquered by the Babylonians.
166	Maccabean Revolt: new Jewish state.

AD

70	Jerusalem and the Temple destroyed by the Romans.
132–135	Jewish revolt under Bar Kochba; Rome's victory.
351	Jewish revolt.
438	Empress Eodicea allows the Jews to return to the Temple Mount at Jerusalem.
614	Persian Empire.
628	Byzantine period.
633–637	Arabic (Islamic) takeover; Jewish attempt to reestablish their state.

Interim period: An Islamic period.

1099–1291	The Crusades directed toward the Holy Land.
1187	Salah Ed-din restores Islam in most parts of the land.
1244	Kharegmians (Ghengis Khan).
1260	Mamelucs.
1260	Mongolian attempt to regain power.
1517–1917	Ottoman Empire—Turkey (400 years over the whole land).

The 20th Century

1897
The first Zionist congress held in Basel.

1917–1920
Area under British military control.

1920–1948
British Mandate. The British Empire defeats the Turks (the Ottomans) 1917 and gets the Holy Land in return.

1917
The British issue the Balfour Declaration by which the Jews are promised possession of Palestine.

1919
The British are commissioned by the League of Nations (forerunner of UN), to restore Palestine as a Jewish state. Desire for oil shapes British foreign policy.

1921
75% of the Palestine Mandate becomes an Arab state—Trans Jordan.

1947
The British leave Palestine without successfully resolving the Arab-Israeli question. The UN suggests a partition plan of the remaining areas. Three disconnected areas, excluding Jerusalem, are given to the Jews and three to the Arabs. Only the Jews accept the plan.

14 May 1948
Cessation of the British Mandate. The Jews declare their independence and establish their state—Israel.

15 May 1948
The War of Independence. Egypt, Syria, Iraq and Lebanon attack the newfound state.

3 June 1949
A cease-fire is declared. Israel's area is now somewhat larger than the UN's partition plan. Jordan occupies Samaria and Judea (the West Bank) and holds this area

for 19 years. The Sinai area that Israel had taken is returned in the 1949 peace negotiations. Sinai was not Egyptian territory, but was under Egyptian military administration, as had the Gaza area.

1956

Egypt nationalizes the Suez Canal. The British and French attack Egypt. Egypt recruits the Fedayin (Palestinian/Arabs) to perform terrorist attacks against Israeli civilian targets Israel joins forces with the allies in an attempt to stop Egyptian terrorism. Israel takes Gaza and Sinai but has to return them in accordance with the cease fire agreement. UN peacekeeping forces are placed in the area.

1964

The PLO is founded in Cairo by Egypt, Syria and Iraq. Its aim—to fight Israel.

1967

The Six Day War. Nasser closes the international waterway, the Gulf of Aquaba, thereby hindering Israel's trade with Africa via Eilat. Israel has already made it known that such action would not be tolerated and therefore attacks Egypt. On the first day, half of Egypt's airforce rendered inoperable. When UN's peacekeeping forces leave Sinai, Egyptian forces are already at Israel's border.

Syria reinforces the Golan Heights, already thought to be impregnable. At Gennesaret they had hills of 1,200–1,300 feet and in the north at Mt. Hermon, 8,500 feet. Israelis are subjected to continual terror and consequently, children live in bunkers up to 1967. Israel is at first defensive in the north east against Syria, but on the third day, after Egyptian pressure eases, she attacks Syria. Israel had promised not to attack Jordan if she withdrew from involvement. However, on the second day, Jordan attacks Jerusalem. Israel retaliates and Iraq supports Jordan. Cooperation of Arab countries—Saudi Arabia, the Arab Emirates, Libya, Algeria and Morocco with help from Soviet military advisors. On the fourth day Israel successfully invades East Jerusalem. Israel has now gained the Golan Heights, Samaria, Judea (the West Bank), the Sinai Peninsula and East Jerusalem.

August 1967
The Arab lands hold a convention in Khartoum and formulate their relationship with Israel, to be based on three negative principles:
1. No peace with Israel,
2. No negotiations with Israel,
3. No recognition of Israel.

1969–1970
War of Attrition along the Suez.

October 1973
Yom Kippur War. An organized attack against Israel, whose army was largely demobilized during the Feast of Tabernacles. At first it was 1 Israeli against 20 Syrians, 70 Israeli tanks against Syria's 1200. Jordan avoids fighting but supports the Arabs. After 3–4 weeks, Israel has the advantage. After the war Israel gains more land.

1979
Peace Treaty with Egypt under which Israel surrenders the Sinai Peninsula piecemeal by 1982.

1980
Israel bombs a nuclear power plant in Iraq to stop production of atomic bombs.

1982
Israel invades southern Lebanon and surrounds Beirut. Her aim—to crush the PLO's headquarters, seize weapons and make an end to the incessant attacks against the North Galilee area.

December 1987
The Intifada starts.

1991
Iraq attacks Israel.

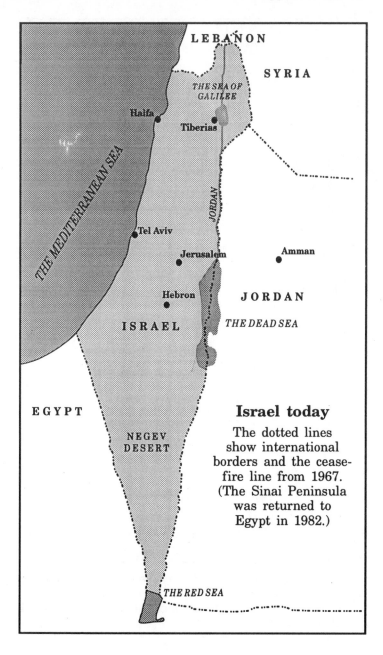

Israel today

The dotted lines show international borders and the cease-fire line from 1967. (The Sinai Peninsula was returned to Egypt in 1982.)

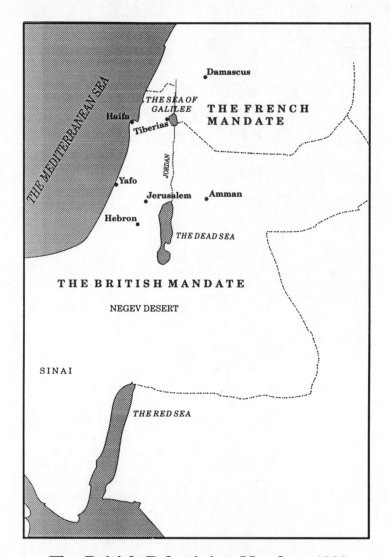

The British Palestinian Mandate 1922

The original Mandate, accorded by the Balfour Declaration, was to be the Jewish homeland. But this was divided into Trans Jordan and a smaller Palestinian Mandate, which ended in 1948.

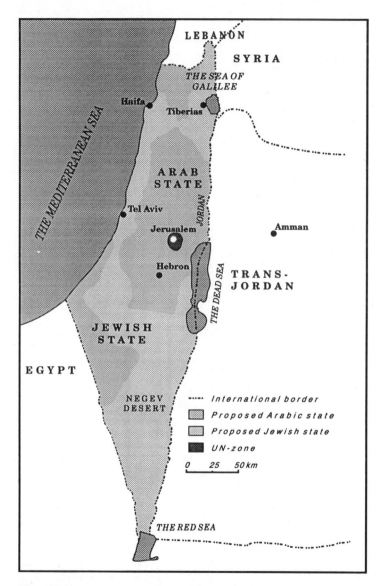

The UN's partition vote, which divided the Palestinian Mandate into Jewish and Arab States, was accepted by the Jews but rejected by the Arabs.

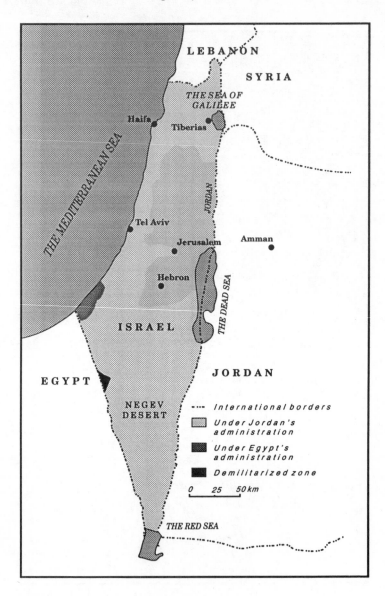

After the State of Israel was declared, five armies attacked them. The war ended with Israel receiving a larger area.

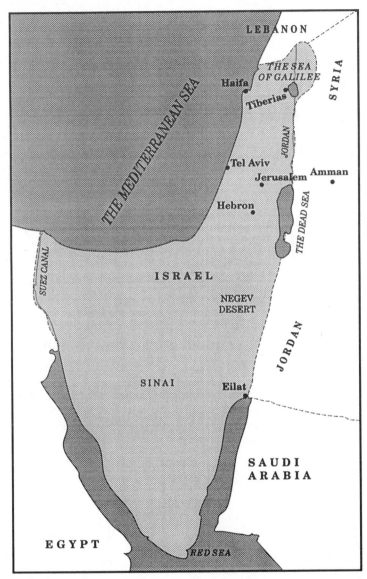

Israel, immediately after the Six-Day War of 1967: having taken the Golan heights, the West Bank, Sinai and East Jerusalem.

Jewish Immigration in Modern History

1882–1903	approx. 20,000–30,000
1904–1914	approx. 35,000–40,000
1919–14/5 1948	482,857
15/5 1948–1951	686,739
1952–1954	54,065
1955–1957	164,936
1958–1960	75,487
1961–1964	228,046
1965–1968	81,337
1969–1971	116,484
1972–1974	142,755
1975–1979	124,827
1980–1984	83,637
1985–1988	46,146
1989	24,050
1/1–30/9 1990	112,688
1/1–30/11 1990	approx. 150,000 from the USSR

The increase in Jewish immigration to Palestine during the 1900's was accompanied by an increase in Arab immigration. The original Arab population was not as large as Arabs contest today.

Population

Jews	81.7%
Muslims	14.2%
Christians	2.3%
Druze and others	1.8%

Of a population of 4,477,000 (Judea, Samaria and Gaza excluded), 3,659,000 are Jews, while 818,000 represent Muslims, Christians, Druze and others.

Glossary

Aliya	Wave of Jewish immigration to Palestine/Israel
Anti-Semitism	Enmity towards Jews
Assimilate	Integration
Diaspora	Dispersion of the Jews
Nablus	Shechem
PAMJAT	Anti-Semitic movement in former USSR (CIS)
PLO	Palestinian Liberation Organization
Palestine	British Mandate 1917–1948. Modern Israel and Jordan together. The name is reminiscent of the ancient Philistines, who were once Israel's most hostile enemy
Palestinian	Arab who has lived in Palestine for at least two years before 1948
Zionism	The movement founded by Theodor Herzel, for the purpose of reestablishing the Jews in their ancient homeland: Zion
Shema	The Jewish faith confession (Deut 6)
The West Bank	Samaria and Judea

BY ULF EKMAN

A Life of Victory
The Authority in the Name of Jesus
Destroy the Works of the Devil
Faith that Overcomes the World
Financial Freedom
God, the State and the Individual
God Wants to Heal Everyone
Tehe Power in the New Creation
The Prophetic Ministry